GOD of MEDICINE

Dr. Sabelo Sam Gasela Mhlanga

GOD
OF
MEDICINE

Dr. Sabelo Sam Gasela Mhlanga

ISBN: 979-8-9899221-5-4 Paperback
ISBN: 979-8-9899221-6-1 Hardback

Independently Published by: Dr Sabelo Sam Mhlanga

Because of the dynamic nature of the Internet, any web addresses or links contained in this book may have changed since publication and may no longer be valid. The views expressed in this work are solely those of the author and do not necessarily reflect the views of the publisher, and the publisher hereby disclaims any.

TABLE OF CONTENTS

CHAPTER FOUR

CHAPTER FIVE

CHAPTER SIX

CHAPTER SEVEN

CHAPTER EIGHT

PREFACE

The saga of my expertise is woven from countless narratives of triumph over adversity. It is a tale that began in the humble halls of academia, where the seeds of curiosity were sown, germinating into a lifelong quest for knowledge. Yet, this journey has been anything but linear. Challenges, both profound and perplexing, have been constant companions. From battling the specters of disease in under-resourced communities to navigating the labyrinthine corridors of global health policy, every trial has been a crucible, refining my resolve and honing my insights. These experiences, as harrowing as they were, illuminated the path to a deeper understanding of the intrinsic link between body, mind, and spirit in the healing process. My accolades, while numerous, are not the sum of my contributions but rather the byproducts of a relentless pursuit of healing and understanding.

Medicine is a compound that is used to treat or prevent diseases in a form or drug or drugs, in substance or powder forms, and tablets. It is the science or practice of the diagnosis, treatment, and prevention of diseases. Pathology and medicine have been part of the beginning of humanity. By nature, God designed medicine to help humans boost their immunity and heal and cure their bodies from illnesses, diseases, and plagues. God created vegetation for human survival, using the bark of trees, roots, and leaves of various trees to soothe and cure diseases. Natural elements of vegetation are available and are at human disposal for their survival on earth. In the same vein, God uses supernatural phenomena to heal with his supernatural power, which is often called miraculous events, when the divine evades the natural. In this book, I will argue the fact that God uses both, the natural medicine, and the divine healing to accomplish human health.

This book is dedicated to my lovely wife, Judith Gasela Mhlanga and our four children, Blessing Qhawe, Shalom Sinqobile, Emmanuel Nkosi, Prosper Thando, and Joseph Sam Nkosana. My wife Judith, my daughter Shalom, and I are working in health systems and with health backgrounds in our degrees. I work in both health systems and spiritual departments. It is in that context that I write this book to have encountered and experienced patients and church members receiving healing on these two fronts. At the University of Washington Medicine, I work as a clinical and spiritual professional and the experience has enhanced my deeper understanding of how vital both medicine and spirituality play in the lives of the patients. By the same token, as a minister of the gospel, I have witnessed God, miraculously healing some people with various diseases, disabilities, ailments, depression, schizophrenia, bipolar disorders, and many various human health challenges.

INTRODUCTION

In the realm of healing, where science and spirituality intersect, few have trodden as confidently or with as much reverence as I have. My name, Dr. Sabelo Sam Gasela Mhlanga, might resonate across the corridors of medical institutions, echo within the sanctuaries of spiritual assemblies, or be found gracing the citations of pioneering research papers. My journey has not been one of mere academic pursuit, but a pilgrimage of profound healing, grounded in the wisdom of both science and faith.

With decades spent at the helm of medical innovation, interfacing as a Minister, Professor, and Clinical Counselor, my voyage through medicine and spirituality has been marked by an unyielding commitment to the sanctity of life. My credentials, stretching across esteemed positions and groundbreaking research, serve not as mere accolades but as milestones in a relentless quest for truth and healing.

Medicine is a compound used to treat or prevent diseases in the form of drugs or substances or powder forms. It is the science or practice of diagnosing, treating, and preventing diseases. Pathology and medicine have been part of the beginning of humanity. By nature, God designed medicine to help humans boost their immunity and heal and cure their bodies from illnesses, diseases, and plagues. God created vegetation for human survival, using the bark of trees, roots, and leaves of various trees to soothe and cure diseases. Natural elements of vegetation are available and are at human disposal for their survival on earth. In the same vein, God uses supernatural phenomena to heal with his supernatural power, which is often called miraculous events, when the divine evades the natural. In this book, I will argue the fact that God uses both, natural medicine, and divine healing to accomplish human health. "Medicine is the science and practice of caring for a patient, managing the diagnosis, prognosis, prevention, treatment, palliation of injury or disease, and promoting their health."[1]

The book explores natural and modern medicine and how medicine affects both cities and communal lands. There has been a controversy for many centuries about natural medicine and modern medicine. The natural medicine that is referred to in this book is medicine in the form of roots, leaves, stems, barks, herbs, and seeds, without being processed through machinery to be in the form of power and preserved. Natural medicine is tapped from the ground, trees, leaves, roots, herbs, and seeds. Natural medicine is prescribed through herbalists, and common knowledge by parents and community residents about certain herbs that are good for stomach aches, headaches, pneumonia, nausea, cold, flu, or a broken leg or broken arm. There is no accurate dosage but whoever is a practitioner knows how much is too much or low dosage. In contrast to natural medicine, there is modern medicine that is prescribed by physicians, and prescriptions are accessed through pharmacies in the cities and towns. Modern medicine is regarded as credible, authentic, relevant, and produced by modern factories and pharmacies.

The book will explore Biblical Medicine and how God instructed the prophets or his servants to administer healing to certain people using herbs, seeds, soil, leaves, or roots. Let us explore together the mind of God about healing through natural herbs as the God of medicine. My dedication to medicine and spirituality is not born out of ambition alone but is deeply rooted in a personal saga of loss and redemption. Witnessing the ravages of illness within my

---

[1] Medicine-Wikipedia, http://en.m.wikipedia.org, (Accessed December 3, 2024).

own family, I was confronted with the limitations of conventional medicine and the profound power of faith and holistic healing. This duality, this intersection of science and spirituality, became my battlefield and my sanctuary. It is a narrative that resonates with the universal human experience of suffering and the quest for solace, making my engagement with medicine a deeply personal crusade.

This book, therefore, is not merely a recounting of professional triumphs or a catalog of medical innovations. It is an invitation to journey alongside me, through the valleys of despair and the peaks of revelation, to uncover the essence of true healing. It is a call to arms, challenging the conventional paradigms of medicine and advocating for a more holistic, spiritually informed approach to healing.

Imagine, if you will, a world where medicine transcends the physical, where healers are not only adept in the science of the body but are also custodians of the soul. This is the world I envision, and through the pages of this book, I invite you to explore the possibilities of such a reality. Together, we stand at the cusp of a new dawn in medicine, one where the God of Medicine is not a deity distant and detached but a presence, deeply ingrained in the very fabric of healing.

In this book, amidst tales of innovation and introspection, I offer not just knowledge but wisdom, not just solutions but solace. It is a manifesto for the modern healer, a beacon for those weary from the journey, and a testament to the indomitable spirit of those who dare to dream of a world healed not just in body, but in spirit.

Welcome, then, to this consortium of enlightenment, where the art of healing is reimagined and where each page turned is a step closer to the divine. Together, let us embark on this sacred pilgrimage, for in the pursuit of healing, we find not just the God of Medicine, but the very essence of our humanity.

As I stand at the confluence of these diverse streams of knowledge, I am reminded of that pivotal moment from my childhood. The spark of compassion that was ignited beside a dusty road in Zimbabwe has grown into a blazing torch, guiding me through the shadows of doubt and despair.

"God of Medicine" is not merely a title or a book; it is a calling. It is a promise to those who suffer that they are not alone, that their pain is heard, and that healing, in its most holistic sense, is possible. This book is an invitation to you, dear reader, to join me in exploring the vast landscapes of healing, where science and spirituality walk hand in hand.

CHAPTER ONE
GOD OF MEDICINE & HEALING

THE SPARK OF COMPASSION

In the heart of Zimbabwe, where the earth breathes the tales of generations and the sky stretches wide and clear, my journey found its first whisper of destiny. It was here, amid the rugged beauty of my homeland, that a single moment pivoted my life towards a path I had never imagined, leading me to become Dr. Sabelo Sam Gasela Mhlanga, a name now synonymous with the harmonious blend of medicine and spirituality.

I was only ten years old when I was ignited by a spark of compassion for human health and spirituality. The sun hung heavily that day, painting the horizon in hues of gold and amber, as I stumbled upon a scene that would forever alter the course of my life.

My journey into counseling and spiritual ministry was an expansion. It was an acknowledgment that true healing transcends the physical, touching upon the emotional and spiritual wounds that all too often lie at the heart of our ailments.

Countless encounters with the miracles of medical healing have marked the road I have traveled on. I have seen lives transformed, not just by the medicines and procedures of modern science but by the ancient practices that honor the interconnectedness of all life, infusing it with a sense of awe and humility.

In the realm of healing, where the tangible meets the intangible, Dr. Sabelo Sam Gasela Mhlanga found his true calling. His journey, deeply engraved with the scars and triumphs of those he sought to heal, ventured beyond the realms of conventional medicine. It spiraled into the essence of faith, a component as crucial to his practice as the stethoscope slung around his neck. Faith, a term often tossed around in the whirlwinds of daily conversations held a profound significance for Dr. Mhlanga. But what is faith? At its core, faith is the complete trust or confidence in someone or something, often not based on something unseen and the substance of things hoped for, the evidence of things, not sin, (Hebrews 11:1). In the context of Dr. Mhlanga's life, it was the unwavering belief in the unseen forces of healing, the conviction that there exists a higher power guiding the hands of those who heal.

THE INFLUENCE OF FAITH

Diving deeper, faith for Dr. Mhlanga wasn't merely a belief in divine intervention. It was the acknowledgment of the intricate dance between mind, body, and spirit in the healing process. This recognition wasn't born out of thin air. It was the culmination of years of observation, learning, and, most importantly, experiencing the limits of medicine when it came to healing the whole person.

Historically, the concept of faith is rooted that burrow deep into the origins of human civilization. From the shamanistic rituals of ancient tribes to the prayerful meditations of modern religions, faith has always played a pivotal role in humanity's quest for healing. Dr. Mhlanga's understanding of faith, however, was not confined to religious dogma. It was broader, encompassing the faith in oneself, in the patient, and in the collective human capacity to overcome adversity. Faith, a term often tossed around in the whirlwinds of daily conversations held a profound significance for Dr. Mhlanga. But what is faith? At its core, faith is the complete trust or confidence in someone or something, often not based on something unseen and the substance of things hoped for, the evidence of things, not sin, (Hebrews 11:1). In the context of Dr. Mhlanga's life, it was the unwavering belief in the unseen forces of healing, the conviction that there exists a higher power guide thing the hands of those who heal.

Placing this concept within a broader framework of medical anthropology, biblical counseling, clinical/spiritual care, and ministry. Dr. Mhlanga saw faith as the bridge connecting the empirical world of medicine with the ethereal realm of spiritual healing. In real-world applications, this belief manifested in his approach to patient care. He treated everyone not as a case study but as a unique narrative, a confluence of stories that needed understanding and empathy as much as diagnoses and treatments.

The misconception that faith and medicine are mutually exclusive couldn't be further from the truth, a notion Dr. Mhlanga dedicated his life to dispelling. He often encountered skepticism, the raised eyebrows of colleagues who viewed his methods as unconventional, if not outright unscientific. Yet, time and again, the results spoke volumes.

To put everything in good perspective and to coin God of Medicine in his creation and all the vegetation and all that is in it, both animals and the forest. Before God man and female in his image and likeness, he created the universe, vegetation, animals, reptiles, insects, fish, all the living things, and finally, human beings, *Adama*. Then God said, "Let Us make man in Our image, according to Our likeness; let them have dominion over the fish of the sea, over the birds of the air, and over the cattle, over all the earth and over every creeping thing that creeps on the earth." So, God created man in His image; in the image of God, He created him; male and female He created them. Then God blessed them, and God said to them, "Be fruitful and multiply; fill the earth and subdue it; have dominion over the fish of the sea, over the birds of the air, and over every living thing that moves on the earth." And God said, "See, I have given you every herb *that* yields seed which *is* on the face of all the earth, and every tree whose fruit yields seed; to you it shall be for food. Also, to every beast of the earth, to every bird of the air, and to everything that creeps on the earth, in which *there is* life, *I have given* every green herb for food"; and it was so. Then God saw everything that He had made, and indeed *it was* very good. So, the evening and the morning were the sixth day, (Genesis 1:26-31, NKJV).

We must make it plain clear that God has set the universe in motion and the earth, and he owns everything in it. He gave man the authority to rule and to subdue everything in it. God created all things by his command; however, when God made man, as the crown of his handiwork, there was a dialogue within the Godhead. For God to create man at the end of all creation was an honor and favor. Before man was created, God filled the earth with vegetation and animals, a provision for man's survival. God created man with wisdom, unlike any created animals before him. The verse brings in the divine revelation of Trinity. When God was creating, He said, "Let there be . . ." but when man was made, God made a consultation: "Let us make man in Our *image*, according to Our *likeness*." In creating the universe, vegetation and animals, God used authority and command, but it was with affection that he created man. The three persons of the Trinity consulted and concurred to make man. Mathews asserts,

The creation account shows an ascending order of significance with human life as the final, thus pinnacle, creative acts, this is the only one preceded by divine deliberation ("Let us make" in v. 26). This expression replaces the impersonal words spoken in the previous creation acts, (e.g. "Let there be," "Let the earth").[2]

---

[2]Kenneth A. Mathews, *Genesis 1-11:26*, The New American Commentary, vol. 1A (Nashville: Broadman & Holman, 1996), 160.

Mathews drives the point that human life alone is special in the sight of God because man was created in the image of God and has a special place in creation.

Man was made in God's image and after his likeness. These two words express the same thing about *imago Dei*. When verse 26 is examined closer, the interpretation of plural pronouns "let us," "our image," and our "likeness" draw attention to the identity of the Creator. Mathews continues,

Regarding the verb "make," we have already observed at 1:1 that the verbs "made" (*asa*) and "created" (*bara*) are in parallel both structurally and semantically in 2.4a, b. Here the parallel between v.26 ("Let us make") and v.27 ("So God created") indicates that they are virtual synonyms.[3]

The dialogue within the Godhead displays divine honor in creating human life. Gordon J. Wenham explains, "It refers to the 'fullness of attributes and powers conceived as united within the Godhead.'"[4] One would concur with the suggestion that it is the plural of fullness.

God blessed Adam and Eve and said, "Be fruitful and multiply' fill the earth and subdue it; have dominion over the fish of the sea, over the birds of the air, and over every living thing that moves on the earth." God gave the human family the privilege and responsibility of taking care of all creation. As sin entered the earth, it negatively affected the prosperity of the earth and all living things in it.

God gave Adam and Eve two assignments: procreation and dominion. To all animals, God gave power to reproduce themselves. In Mesopotamia and Canaan, creation motifs were linked to fertility rites, and Genesis 1:28, NKJV, puts that concept to rest. Reproduction is a God-given blessing and gift, which is not dependent on rites

---

[3]Ibid.
[4]Gordon J. Wenham, *Genesis 1-15*, Word Biblical Commentary, vol. 1 (Waco, TX: Word, 1987), 28.

devoted to gods or idols. The purpose of God giving man a mandate to multiply and fill the earth was so that man would rule over the animals. God gave Adam and Eve a divine purpose for marriage: the procreation of children. It is God's purpose, will, and desire to bless his people with children and fill the earth. The blessing of God to be "fruitful" and "fill" the earth is the source from which humans emanate. John Calvin writes,

But here Moses would simply declare that Adam with his wife was formed to produce offspring so that men might replenish the earth. God could have himself indeed have covered the earth with a multitude of men; but it was his will that we should precede from one fountain, so that our desire of mutual concord might be the greater, and that each might the more freely embrace the other as his flesh.[5]

In the same vein, it is in God's power, within his will and purpose, to allow some to be fruitful and others be barren. This barrenness might be the result of a medical condition, biological complication, or simply the will of the Lord. God is Sovereign, and He does what He wants for special purposes.

The man was created as God's representative on earth. Man is the crown of God's creation, and he has a special mandate bestowed on him by God. He is accountable for everything on earth in the sky, the land, the waters, the animals, and to other human beings, to be his "brother's keeper." God mandated man to rule and subdue all the living creatures of the sky, of the land, and of the water. Air and water pollution, land deforestation, and the killing of creatures to use their flesh as food were not mandated. It was after the flood that domination in the consumption of

---

[5]John Calvin, *Commentary on Genesis*, *Commentaries on the First Book of Moses*, vol. 1 (Grand Rapids: Baker, 1996), 97.

animals was extended to man (Gen 9:3). Hamilton propounds,

Of the two verbs, *rada*, "exercise dominion," and *kaba*, "subdue," the later connotes more force. Thus it refers to subjecting someone to slavery (2 Chr 28:10; Neh 5:5; Jer 34:11, 16), to physical abuse. All these references suggest violence or a display of force. For reasons already indicated, it appears unlikely that we need to transfer the nuance of force and dictatorship into the use of *kabas* in Gen 1:28.[6]

Humankind should treat animals with dignity and take care of the environment, including water, air, and land. All creation was to be subdued by man as God's representative and God gave humankind power to rule: "This is a place in which God has set man to be the servant of his providence in the government of the creatures, and, as it were, the intelligence of the of this orb, to be the receiver of God's bounty, which other creatures live upon."[7] Fruitfulness is dependent on God the creator. The Hebrew tradition was that love for the earth was sacred and human righteousness related to the welfare of the earth. "A righteous man regraded the life of his beast: ..." (Prov 12:10a; 27:23; Deut 25:4, KJV). The medicine that God gave to man's disposal to use for his healing and survival. However, the man was also responsible for using the medicine wisely, not to harm himself with the medicine. The free will that God gave to man was to exercise prudence, intellect, and wisdom which is the application of knowledge. There was a mutual relationship and harmony between God and man before sin entered humanity through Satan's deception. God commanded, "Of every tree the garden you may freely eat; but of the tree of the knowledge of good and evil you shall not eat, for in the day that you eat of it you shall surely die" (Gen 2:16-17, NKJV). God alone knows

---

[6]Hamilton, *The Book of Genesis*, 139.
[7]Ibid., 140.

what is good for man. For man to enjoy the "good," man must trust and obey God in every word that he spoke/speaks. When man disobeys God, he decides for himself what is good and bad.

One particularly vivid example was the case of a young girl, wracked with an illness that left her bedridden and isolated. Where medicine had drawn its last card, Dr. Mhlanga's faith played its hand. Through a combination of medical treatment and spiritual counseling, slowly but surely, the girl regained not just her physical strength but also a will to live that had been eroded by months of suffering.

In moments like these, faith revealed its true influence. It was the beacon that guided lost souls back to the shore of health and well-being. It was the light that pierced through the darkest despair, offering hope where none seemed possible.

So, what is the essence of faith in medicine? It is the understanding that healing is a journey of the body, guided by the mind and uplifted by the spirit. It is recognition that, within the complex machinery of human biology, there lies a spark of the divine, waiting to be ignited by the warmth of compassion and empathy.

This narrative, this exploration of faith's role in the healing arts, is not just Dr. Mhlanga's story. It's an invitation to all who wield the tools of medicine to look beyond the symptoms, to see the patient in their entirety, and to embrace the potent blend of science and spirituality.

As the sun sets on another day in the life of Dr. Mhlanga, one can't help but wonder: How many more lives will be touched by his unique blend of medicine and faith? How many more souls will find solace in their holistic approach to healing?

The answers lie ahead, woven into the fabric of countless stories yet to unfold. But one thing remains clear: In the intricate dance of healing, faith is not just a spectator;

it's a partner, moving gracefully to the rhythm of life's most profound mysteries.

God has been revered across cultures and ages as the ultimate healer and the source of all medicinal knowledge. The divine connection to healing manifests through nature, wisdom, and the harmonious balance of creation. The concept of the "God of Medicine" represents a being who embodies both the wisdom of curing ailments and the compassionate desire to alleviate suffering.

In many ancient traditions, medicine and healing were considered sacred arts, entrusted to individuals believed to be chosen by God. These healers acted as intermediaries, channeling divine energy and knowledge to restore health. This connection is reflected in symbols like the caduceus, which is associated with healing and medicine.

The role of the God of Medicine extends beyond physical healing to include mental, emotional, and spiritual well-being. It emphasizes that true healing is holistic, addressing the individual. This divine aspect serves as a reminder that medicine is not merely a science but also an art imbued with compassion and ethics.

Understanding the God of Medicine means recognizing the interconnectedness of all life. Humans, animals, and ecosystems are part of a delicate balance, and healing one often necessitates understanding and preserving the others. The divine essence inspires humanity to innovate and explore while remaining rooted in the principles of care, balance, and harmony.

GOD THE CREATOR OF ALL MEDICINE

God put man in charge of the earth and everything in it. The medicine that man can manufacture according to his wisdom and knowledge, God authorized the mandate, and he works in partnership with God. Scriptures reveal that the image and likeness of God remained in man even after the fall. As a royal representative of God, man is still the only crown of life of God's creation. Genealogy is the perpetuation of the original:

This is the book of the genealogy of Adam. On the day that God created man, He made him in the likeness of God. He created them male and female and blessed them and called them Mankind in the day they were created. And Adam lived one hundred and thirty years, and begot a son in his likeness, after his image, and named him Seth, (Gen 5:1-3).[8]

Being the original created being in the image and likeness of God and representing God, God commanded Adam to procreate with Eve for his offsprings resembling him. Man can utilize his abilities and capabilities to survive the ailments that he suffers in the form of diseases, infections, injuries, and natural disasters.

Reflecting upon an illness or injury episode in relation to "Biomedicine," "Ethnomedicine," and/or health disparities, it is imperative to understand the various patterns that emerge when people find themselves sick. It is common knowledge that when people get sick, they find alternative ways to determine and use various knowledge to find solutions. Biomedicine is defined as "the healing practice in specific cultures."[9] It is imperative to understand the dynamics of cultures and their belief systems in relation to

---

[8]Leupold, *Exposition of Genesis*, 184.

[9] Seth, Messinger, *ANTH 215 A*, Lecture 3, 22, 2018, p. 21.

sickness, medication, and prevention. The tapping of local and indigenous knowledge and material that is effective in diagnosis, treatment and care is fundamental in medical anthropology. Ethnomedicine is defined as the "healing practices followed by a specific or particular people identified as a culture."[10]

People in particular cultures have their own understanding about the healing processes and medical procedures. Therefore, ethnomedicine defines a particular culture with its own medical and care system. Each culture is unique and follows its methodologies to achieve curing and healing practices. The definition of these terms has not changed but they have been expounded over the years since the world has become a global village. As a result, ethnomedicine, biomedicine and health disparities have elucidated extensively to add the meanings of the terms according to the context of the culture. "Medical anthropology seeks to understand the experience of sufferers to illuminate the human dimension of illness and health dynamics."[11] Good asserts, "Western curing is aimed exclusively at the mechanical body, while Zinacanteco procedures are directed at social relations and supernatural agents."[12]

It means healthcare disparities focus on some members of the community who can and cannot access healthcare services and facilities. Socioeconomics will, in most cases, disadvantage those who have disabilities and those who are poor. The health disparities can prevent opportunities for those who have diseases, injuries, violence, or other illnesses if they are not reviews for unequal benefits

---

[10] Ibid. p. 17.
[11] Ibid. p. 9.
[12] Bryan J. Good, *Medicine, Rationality and Experience*, (New York: University of Cambridge Press, 1994), 27.

because of social status. "Sickness" is a feeling of not well. This is not limited to body not functioning normally, but it includes emotional, psychological, and mental imbalance. According to Hugh and Lock, "Sickness is a form of communication through which nature, social and culture speak..."[13] According to Singer and Baer, "Disease and illness are the result of biological processes. It exists within a cultural framework. Disease is the disruption in the dynamic 'steady state' of the body. Disease is a maladaptive state of body."[14] The causes of illnesses and diseases varies from place to place. The examples are those from Yanomamo who believe that "Illnesses are caused by ghosts or spirit possessions, the Azande who believe that illness is caused by possession and sorcery, while other cultures believe that illnesses or diseases are caused by environmental imbalance (humoral system)."[15]

Experiential health, which leads to feelings of tranquility and fulfillment, is the goal for functional health. Biomedicine, ethnomedicine, and health disparities bring curing and or healing within the cultural systems of individuals according to their culture. Some of the concepts presented in the class are congruent with my belief system. I believe that health care should be grounded in scientific rationales although community-shared experiences should be given space to explore local and indigenous knowledge for healthcare systems. I see the body as a coherent whole but made up of different parts as a puzzle that fits together to make one beautiful community. Medicine, in its most profound sense, is the divine gift that transcends species and

---

[13] Scheper, Hugh, and Lock, *ANTH 215 A*, Lecture 1, 2018, p.33.

[14] Messinger, *ANTH 215 A*, Lecture 3, January 22 and 24, 2018, p. 2,3,4.

[15] Messinger, Lecture 3, 22, 224, 2018, p. 8

ecosystems. God, as the creator, imbued the natural world with an inherent ability to heal and sustain itself. From the intricate designs of the human body to the vast and interconnected ecosystems of the Earth, divine wisdom is evident in every aspect of life.

Humans have long sought remedies within nature, discovering the medicinal properties of plants, minerals, and other elements provided by God. This pursuit reflects humanity's role as stewards of creation, tasked with understanding and utilizing these divine gifts responsibly. Animals, too, demonstrate an innate understanding of healing, often seeking out specific plants or behaviors to address their ailments, further showcasing the universal reach of God's medicinal provisions.

Ecosystems, as extensions of divine creation, operate as self-sustaining networks of life. They provide air, water, and nutrients essential for health and healing. The balance within these systems mirrors the holistic approach to medicine—where every component has a purpose and a role in the greater good. When ecosystems thrive, they offer a wealth of resources, from oxygen-producing forests to the biodiversity that fuels medical discoveries.

The interdependence between humans, animals, and ecosystems is a testament to God's intricate design. By protecting and nurturing these relationships, humanity aligns itself with divine intentions, fostering a world where healing and well-being are universally accessible.

SPACE AND TELEPATHY

The vast expanse of space has always been a realm of divine mystery and inspiration, symbolizing the boundless nature of God's creation. Space, with its countless stars and galaxies, embodies the infinite wisdom and creativity of the Creator. It represents not only physical dimensions but also the metaphysical connections that transcend human understanding.

Telepathy, often seen as a divine or spiritual gift, underscores the interconnectedness of all beings. This ability to communicate beyond words and physical presence hints at the higher faculties endowed by God to humanity. Telepathy aligns with the belief that thoughts and intentions carry energy, capable of reaching others across vast distances. This phenomenon serves as a reminder of the unseen forces that govern the universe, bridging the gap between the material and spiritual realms.

Space exploration has led humanity to marvel at the intricate balance and design of the cosmos. It has also inspired a deeper understanding of life's interconnectedness. In this vast universe, telepathic connections highlight how individuals and communities are bound by shared consciousness, a divine thread that unites all creation. The concept of telepathy encourages compassion, empathy, and unity, echoing God's intention for harmony among all beings.

In the divine context, space and telepathy symbolize the limitless potential of God's creation and the profound connections that sustain it. They remind humanity of its place in the grand design, urging stewardship, wonder, and reverence for the mysteries that lie beyond.

HUMANS, ANIMALS & ECOSYSTEM

Ethics is the social system adopted by a society or a culture. Ethics depicts the standards or codes of the behavior of a family, a society, or a group of people. Ethics entails choices and actions agreed upon by a group of people, groups, or individuals as norms that would guide a particular person.

Mattingly in her 'moral laboratory' asserts, "The day-to-day experimental living space where moral/ethical are made...Experience is part of time and future decisions and actions are grounded in history."[16] Kleinman propounds, incongruent with Mattingly, "Seen in this light, moral processes differ fundamentally from ethical course. The latter is an abstract articulation and debate over codified value."[17] Experience is a moral process based on societal and ethical codes that are acceptable in a culture. "Mattingly uses 'moral' and 'ethical' exchangeable, distinguishing ethical and moral, universal and moral local."[18] He uses both ethics and morals to assert that all are "working to achieve a socially recognized 'good life' and it is widely shared across cultures (universal)."[19] Kleinman discusses ethics and morals, "Ethical discourse is usually principle-based, with meta-theoretical commentary on the authorization and implication of those principles. (in bioethics, the chief principles are autonomy, beneficence, and justice; they in turn privilege informed consent and confidentiality). Ethical discourse is reflective and intellectualist, emphasizing

---

[16] Cheryl Mattingly, Moral laboratories: Family Peril and the Struggle for Good Life, (Berkeley, CA: University of California, Press, 2014), 35.
[17] Arthur Kleinman, *Experience and its Moral Modes: Culture and Human Conditions and Disorder*, The Tanner Lectures on Human Value, (Stanford University: April 13-16, 1998), 363.
[18] Seth Messinger, Lecture 4, January 29, 2018, p. 29.
[19] Messinger, Lecture 4, 33.

cognition (more precisely, in today's jargon, and rationale choice), over affect or behavior and coherence over the sense of incompleteness and unknowability and uncontrollability that is so prevalent in ordinary life."[20] Drawing from both Mattingly and Kleinman's concepts and the definition of ethics, one would define ethics as social rules/codes adopted by a society to live by. Morals are the personal characteristics of individuals within a society. Therefore, ethics are socially acceptable codes or rules of behavior in society. These sets of rules or principles in society are to curb misconduct and crimes in society.

The common diseases that need immediate attention to be administered with medication using modern medicine include Ebola, Sars, Malaria, COVID-19, and HIV/AIDS. God has given humanity wisdom and knowledge to use medication to heal the populace. The two fundamental prevention and control of diseases are categorized as first in identifying and understanding the nature of the disease such as its mutation, the cause, and the treatment that has been discovered. The second is applying relevant health interventions that are incorporated into education and health systems to curb and prevent the diseases in question. "Anthropology's role conventionally has been in the translation of local concepts of illness and treatment, and the adaptation of biomedical knowledge to fit local aetiologias. Medical anthropology plays an important role in examining the local context of disease diagnosis, treatment, and prevention, and the structural as well as conceptual barriers to improved health status."[21] With recent infectious diseases globally such as Ebola, Sars, Malaria, HIV/AIDS, Covid-19, etc.

---

[20] Kleinman, 363.
[21] National Library of Medicine: *National Center for Biotechnology, Article,* https://pubmed.ncbi.nlm.nih.gov/9892288/, 2018, (Accessed August 30, 2022).

HUMAN DISEASES: EBOLA

Ebola is believed by researchers that it originated from animals such as monkeys, chimpanzees, or fruit bats. It is a virus with various strains that cause Ebola hemorrhagic fever in humans. The symptoms of the disease start like flu, and it progresses rapidly to internal bleeding and organ damage. The virus is transmitted through bodily fluids. The symptoms include fever, sore throat, headaches, diarrhea, bleeding, and muscular pain. The medication applied is Antoltivimab/maftivmab/odesivimab (Inmazeb).

SARS

Severe Acute Respiratory Syndrome (SARS) is a viral respiratory disease caused by SARS which appeared in China in 2002 and spread globally. It is a contagious disease that is a fatal respiratory illness caused by coronavirus. It is transmitted through droplets that enter the air through coughing, sneezing, talking, and breathing from an infected person. The symptoms are dry cough, fever, headaches, muscle aches, and difficulty, breathing. "SARS is an airborne virus and can spread through small droplets of saliva in a similar way to the cold and influenza. It was the first severe and readily transmissible new disease to emerge in the 21st century and showed a clear capacity to spread along the routes of international air travel. SARS can also be spread indirectly via surfaces that have been touched by someone who is infected with the virus."[22] SARS is one of the infectious diseases that rocked the world emanating from Asia. However, it was quickly contained from 2002 to 2004 between the ages of 25 to 70 years old, although some few cases of children under 15 years old appeared here and there.

There is no cure, treatment, or vaccine for SARS but controlling the outbreaks and containing the disease through

---

[22] https://www.who.int/health-topics/severe-acute-respiratory-syndrome#tab=tab_1,.

early detection of cases and isolation, identifying sources of infection, quarantining suspected individuals for ten days, and personal prevention measures.

Malaria

Malaria is caused by a single-celled parasite of the genus Plasmodium. The parasite is transmitted to humans by mosquito bites, a female anopheles. "There are 430 Anopheles mosquito species known around the world, roughly 30 or 4 are vectors (transmitters). The symptoms include fever, chills, headaches, muscle aches, fatigue, nausea, and vomiting diarrhea. The infection can cause kidney failure, seizure, disorientation, coma, and possibly death,"[23] Malaria is transmitted by infected mosquitos, especially, from hot and humid places like Africa and in South America, Eastern Europe, South and Eastern Asia, and in Islands in the Central and South and Pacific Oceans. Malaria is not caused by viruses like other infectious diseases or by bacteria, but it is caused by parasites.

Prevention and Treatment of Malaria

When one is infected by Malaria, it is important to get treatment as soon as possible to kill the parasites. Malaria drugs that are effect include, artemisinin drugs, chloroquine, quinine, atovaquone, Mefloquine and other drugs available. These drugs have proven that they can cure malaria. Those who are planning to travel to visit these areas mentioned above should take preventative medication that may reduce the risks of contracting malaria. One should be aware of and avoid being bitten by mosquitoes. To lower the risks of getting malaria, these are some of the precautions, "Apply mosquito repellent DEET (diethyltoluamide), Drape mosquito netting over beds, Put screens on windows and doors. Treat clothing, mosquito nets, tents, sleeping bags and other fabrics with an insect repellent called permethrin, and

---

[23] https://www.orkin.com, (Accessed August 30, 2022).

wear long pants and long sleeves to cover your skin,"[24] These drugs were developed and tested in Kenya, Ghana, and Malawi as a pilot program to lead on treatment and prevention medication.

HIV/AIDS

HIV/AIDS holds a lot of myths and hypotheses about its origin. It is imperative to understand how and when AIDS came into existence to have adequate information and to know how to deal with this complex disease. According to Sam Puckett and Alan Emery,

"The AIDS virus made its first appearance during the 1960s or earlier in several countries in South Central Africa. The virus is one of a particular class of viruses known as retrovirus… This new form of retrovirus has been named by its various discoveries as "Human T-Lymphotropic Virus Type III" (HTLV-3), "Lymphadenopathy Associated Virus" (LAV), and AIDS Retro Virus (ARV). In 1986 an international science committee gave it the official designation "Human Immuno-deficiency Virus," or "HIV." To the public it is known as "the AIDS virus" and the medical condition it causes is known as "AIDS"—Acquired Immune Deficiency Syndrome."[25]

The AIDS virus is one of the scariest and most feared diseases in human history. HIV/AIDS is an infectious disease caused by the Human Immunodeficiency Virus (HIV). Betty Moffatt explains, Acquired Immune Deficiency Syndrome (AIDS) is the result of a defect in the immune system's family ability to resist certain types of infections: those caused by viruses, fungi, parasites, and mycobacteria (tuberculosis-like organisms). It means that AIDS is not a disease. The mortality rate from AIDS comes

---

[24] https://my.clevelandclinic.org/health/diseases/15014-malaria, (Accessed September 5, 2022).
[25] Sam B. Puckett and Alan R. Emery, *Managing AIDS in the Workplace* (Reading, MA: Addison, 1988), 1.

from the body's inability to resist what is known as 'opportunistic infections.[26]

According to Moffatt, the person dies from the failure of the body's immune system to defend against illnesses: Living with AIDS description of the medical diagnosis of AIDS as affecting the immune system in ways currently under study and revision by researchers...The term "acquired" is used because people with AIDS are known to have normal immune system function before the onset of the syndrome.[27]

---

[26]Betty Clare Moffat, *When Someone You Know Has AIDS: A Book of Hope for Family and Friends* (Santa Monica, CA: IBS, 1986), 34.
[27]Ibid., 35.

CHAPTER TWO

HUMANS, GOD & NATURE

SCRIPTURES ON HERBAL HEALING

Herbal healing is deeply rooted in sacred scriptures and traditions that emphasize the divine wisdom embedded in nature. The Bible, for instance, mentions numerous plants with healing properties, signifying their importance in God's design for human well-being. "The fruit thereof shall be for meat, and the leaf thereof for medicine" (Ezekiel 47:12) highlights the use of plants as a provision for healing.

From ancient times, herbs like frankincense, myrrh, and aloe have been revered not only for their medicinal properties but also for their spiritual significance. Frankincense and myrrh, gifted to the Christ child, symbolize divine healing and protection, while aloe's soothing properties are referenced in the preparation of sacred anointments.

In Ayurveda, a system of medicine rooted in the Indian scriptures, herbs are categorized based on their effects on the body's balance and energy. Similarly, traditional Chinese medicine relies on ancient texts that describe the harmonious use of plants to restore health.

These scriptures serve as a guide to understanding the natural remedies provided by God. They remind humanity of the sacred duty to preserve and respect the earth, recognizing it as a source of sustenance and healing. By aligning with these divine instructions, humanity can access the full potential of herbal medicine to promote health and harmony.

SCRIPTURES ON SOIL HEALING

Healing by touching is one of the most profound expressions of divine healing power. Across cultures and religious traditions, the act of touch has been imbued with spiritual significance, symbolizing both physical and metaphysical connection. In the Bible, the healing touch of Jesus Christ is a central theme, demonstrating the transformative power of divine love and compassion.

One of the most iconic examples of healing by touch is found in the Gospel of Matthew, where a woman suffering from chronic illness reaches out to touch the hem of Jesus's garment. Her faith and the divine power flowing through Jesus heal her instantly. This act illustrates that touch, when combined with faith, can bridge the gap between human frailty and divine strength.

Healing by touch extends beyond religious scripture into practices like Reiki, therapeutic touch, and other holistic modalities. These methods harness the energy within and around the body to promote healing. The practitioner's hands serve as conduits, channeling restorative energy to areas of pain or imbalance.

In the divine context, the power of touch is a reminder of the interconnectedness of all beings. It symbolizes God's closeness and the ability to heal not only the body but also the heart and spirit. The warmth and assurance conveyed through touch affirm the presence of divine care, fostering comfort and hope in times of need.

Educational Pathways

Imagine embarking on a journey, not through the vastness of space or the depths of the ocean, but through the rigorous and often treacherous terrain of medical education. This is the odyssey of Dr. Sabelo Sam Gasela Mhlanga, whose quest to understand the God of Medicine is a testament to resilience, dedication, and an unquenchable thirst for knowledge. The path was neither linear nor easy, fraught with hurdles that would test his resolve at every turn. Yet, Dr. Mhlanga's journey offers a blueprint, a beacon of hope for those daring to follow in his footsteps.

Clinical rotations introduced him to the art of patient care, each encounter a lesson in empathy. It was here, in the crucible of the world, that Dr. Mhlanga's faith intertwined with his scientific knowledge.

Specialization required another leap of faith. Choosing a field meant listening to the whispers of his soul, finding the place where passion and skill met in perfect harmony. Advanced training tested his limits, pushing him to learn, adapt, and grow.

Throughout this journey, practical advice was a lifeline. Mentors urged him to focus, to breathe, to find balance amidst the chaos. They warned of the dangers of burnout, the importance of self-care, and the necessity of maintaining a connection to the way of medicine and faith.

How does one verify the successful completion of this arduous journey? The answer lies not in certificates or accolades, but in the moments of connection with patients, in the lives saved, and in the knowledge passed on to the next generation of healers.

Yet, the path is not without its pitfalls. Doubt, fatigue, and the sheer weight of responsibility can erode even the strongest resolve. Here, the solution lies in the community - in the shared experiences of peers, the wisdom of mentors, and the support of loved ones.

Dr. Mhlanga's journey is a reminder that the road to becoming a clinician is paved with perseverance, sacrifice, and an unwavering commitment to the healing arts. It is a path that few can walk, but for those who do, the rewards are immeasurable.

In moments of reflection, Dr. Mhlanga often pondered the essence of his journey. Was it the countless hours of study, the grueling exams, or the life-and-death decisions that defined his path? Or was it something more, something intangible yet omnipresent, that guided his steps?

The answer, he found, lay in the journey itself. Each step, each stumble, and each triumph were brushstrokes in the masterpiece of his career. For in the heart of Dr. Mhlanga, the God of Medicine was not a title to be earned but a calling to be lived.

So, to those who aspire to walk this path, remember: The journey of a thousand miles begins with a single step. Take that step with courage, with passion, and with the unwavering belief that within you lies the power to heal, to transform, and to inspire.

Mentors and Inspirations

In the tapestry of my career, woven through the fabric of medical science and human empathy, I found that mentors and inspirations were not merely guiding lights but the very essence that propelled me forward. The journey to mastering medical anthropology and global health, to becoming a beacon of hope and healing was illuminated by the wisdom and encouragement of those who had walked the path before me.

This was a place where resources were scarce but compassion was abundant, where each day brought new challenges and opportunities to learn.

The results, though slow to manifest, were nothing short of miraculous. The challenge we faced was monumental.

Reflecting on this time, I realize the depth of what my mentors taught me, that medical anthropology is more than a science; it is an art, a calling that demands knowledge, empathy, patience, and a deep-seated desire to make a difference.

As I ventured further into the realm of the clinical profession, I encountered many more mentors, each leaving an indelible mark on my soul.

These mentors, each unique in their approach, shared a common belief in the power of human connection. They understood that to heal the body, one must first understand the soul.

It means finding your mentors, seeking out those who inspire you, and learning from them. It means embracing the challenges, for it is through overcoming obstacles that we grow. And most importantly, it means never losing sight of the why behind your journey.

As I stand here today, as a minister, a professor, and a clinical counselor, I am a testament to the power of guidance and inspiration. My mentors, with their wisdom and encouragement, helped shape my profession. But the journey does not end with me. It is a path that continues, with each new generation of clinician adding their thread to the tapestry.

So, I leave you with this thought: Who will you inspire? Who will guide you along this noble path? In the realm of medical anthropology and counseling, we are both students and teachers, forever learning, teaching, and embracing empathy.

Under the sterile, white lights of the hospital, where the air smelled of antiseptic solutions and the faint echo of footsteps reverberated off the walls, Dr. Sabelo Sam Gasela Mhlanga took his first steps into what would become his crucible and classroom. Each step was heavy, not just with the weight of his expectations but with the silent prayers of those he aimed to touch.

His first patient, a young boy with eyes as wide as saucers and a mop of hair that defied gravity, lay on the hospital bed, his leg swathed in bandages. The boy's mother, a figure worn by worry, stood by her hands knotted together as if in prayer. Dr. Mhlanga approached with a sense of empathy and trust, his heart thudding in his chest, reminding him of his humanity, his fallibility.

"Will he be alright?" the mother's voice cracked like a whip in the silence, laden with a mix of hope and dread.

Dr. Mhlanga's response was gentle, his voice steady despite the storm of emotions brewing within. "We hope and believe," he assured her, his eyes locking with hers, conveying hope. In our profession, we do not make promises. It also showed him the beauty of the human spirit, the resilience of the body, and the transformative power of empathy. It is a reminder that, in the end, it is our humanity that is our greatest strength.

As you turn the pages of this book, I invite you to walk with me through the corridors of hospitals, to stand beside the beds of the sick and the injured, to witness the miracles wrought by hands guided by knowledge and hearts driven by compassion. For in these stories, you will find not just the art and science of medicine but the very essence of what it means to be human.

So, let's begin. Let us explore together the sacred journey of those who have taken up the call to heal, to comfort, to serve. In their stories, we may just find the wisdom to navigate the complexities of our own lives, to face our own challenges with courage, and to embrace the beauty of our shared humanity.

CHAPTER THREE

WELCOME TO A JOURNEY INTO THE HEART OF MEDICINE.

MEMORABLE PATIENT STORIES

In the dim light of a winter morning, as the sun barely peeked over the horizon, the hospital stood as a beacon of hope in the heart of the city. Its walls, though cold and unyielding, held within them stories of life, death, and the unceasing battle between the two. It was here, amid the ceaseless beeps of machines and the whispers of nurses, that another chapter unfolded chapter that would leave an indelible mark on my heart and reinforce the sacred tenets of my vocation.

The central figures in this narrative were an elderly gentleman of considerable wit and resilience, Mr. Alfred Thompson, and his devoted wife of fifty years, Mrs. Eliza Thompson. Mr. Thompson, a retired teacher, had been battling chronic heart disease, a condition that had gradually eroded his body but not his spirit. His wife, a constant presence by his side, embodied grace and fortitude, her eyes reflecting decades of shared joy and sorrow.

The challenge that confronted us was formidable. Mr. Thompson's condition had taken a turn for the worse, presenting complications that left him teetering on the brink. The prognosis was grim; time, it seemed, was a luxury we could ill afford. The core issue lay not just in extending his life but in ensuring quality in the time he had left. It was a test of our skills, our ethics, and our compassion.

Our approach was multifaceted. It involved a delicate balance of aggressive medical intervention and palliative care, designed to manage his symptoms and alleviate his discomfort. Collaborating closely with a team of specialists, we charted a course that was both bold and cautious, always prioritizing Mr. Thompson's dignity and his family's wishes. It was a dance with the uncertain, each step taken with careful consideration.

The results, though not miraculous, were profoundly impactful. We managed to stabilize Mr. Thompson's condition, granting him precious additional weeks. More importantly, we were able to significantly improve his quality of life during this period. He could share moments of laughter and reflection with his loved ones, imparting wisdom and love that would outlive him.

Reflecting on this case, several insights emerge. First and foremost is the reminder that medicine, at its core, is about people. It's not just prolonging life but enhancing the quality of the time we have. This experience also underscored the importance of communication and collaboration with patients and their families, ensuring that treatment aligns with their values and desires.

While there were no visual aids to encapsulate this journey, the emotional tapestry woven by Mr. Thompson and his family's resilience, love, and grace was vivid. It highlighted the profound impact healthcare professionals can have, not just on the patients under their care but also on the families who love them.

This story connects back to the larger narrative of my career and the essence of this book, the human side of medicine. It serves as a poignant reminder that behind every case number, every diagnosis is a person with hopes, fears, and loved ones. It underscores the responsibility that comes with the white coat: to care, to comfort, and to honor the trust placed in us by those we serve.

As you turn the page, I leave you with a question to ponder: In the face of adversity, what marks the true measure of success? Is it the victories over disease and death, however fleeting they may be, or the ability to touch lives, to ease suffering, and to imbue the remaining moments with dignity and love?

Let us continue our journey, exploring the depths of human resilience and the boundless capacity for compassion that defines the true spirit of medicine.

THE ART OF DIAGNOSIS

The art of diagnosis, a cornerstone of medical anthropology, weaves together the empirical and the intuitive, the scientific and profound human. This intricate process is not merely a task of identifying diseases but a profound exploration of the stories of those we aim to heal. Diagnosis begins with a narrative patient's story, symptoms whispered in the quiet of a consultation room. These initial threads, seemingly disparate, are the first colors in a broader palette. The clinician, much like an artist, must discern patterns within these hues, connecting dots across the vast canvas of medical knowledge.

Understanding the concept of diagnosis requires an appreciation of its dual nature. It is both an art and a science blend of rigorous analysis, pattern recognition, and a dash of intuitive insight. The diagnostic process unfolds in stages, from the gathering of information (the patient's history, physical examination findings) to the formulation and testing of hypotheses through investigations and lab tests. This structured approach is underpinned by a vast body of medical knowledge, yet each step is guided by the clinician's intuition and experience.

Consider, for instance, the case of Anna, a young violinist who presented with intermittent, unexplained joint pain. Initial tests were inconclusive, leading some to suggest a psychological origin. However, a more experienced doctor noted the subtle interplay of symptoms—a pattern mirroring a rare autoimmune disease. Further investigation confirmed the diagnosis, and treatment commenced, offering Anna not just relief but the promise of a normal life. This case exemplifies the diagnostician's challenge: to see beyond the obvious, to listen deeply, and to connect seemingly unrelated dots.

Exploring different perspectives on diagnosis reveals its complexity. Some view it through a purely scientific lens, emphasizing evidence and data. Others adopt a more holistic approach, considering psychological, social, and emotional factors equally important in understanding a patient's condition. This diversity of viewpoints enriches the diagnostic process, ensuring it remains a balanced blend of art and science.

Data and facts are indispensable to diagnosis. They provide the foundation upon which hypotheses are built and tested. For example, the prevalence of certain diseases within specific populations can guide the diagnostician's thinking, suggesting more likely diagnoses based on epidemiological data. However, reliance on data alone is insufficient. The clinician's judgment fills the gaps where data may be sparse or inconclusive.

Complex terms abound in the realm of diagnosis, from 'idiopathic' to 'iatrogenic,' each carrying specific meanings that shape understanding and treatment approaches. Simplifying these terms, idiopathic refers to diseases without a clear cause, while iatrogenic denotes conditions induced by medical treatment itself. Such terms, though complex, are vital in the nuanced discussions between healthcare professionals and in educating patients about their conditions.

In conclusion, the art of diagnosis is a testament to the beauty and complexity of medicine. It requires a delicate balance of science and intuition, of data and personal judgment. Through examples like Anna's, we see the profound impact of a well-crafted diagnosis—not just in identifying a disease but in charting a course toward healing. The key takeaways for any reader, whether a medical professional or simply someone fascinated by the intricacies of healthcare, revolve around the appreciation of this balance. It's about recognizing that behind every diagnosis is a story, a person, and a life profoundly affected by the words spoken in the aftermath of discovery.

Diagnosis, then, is more than a label; it is the first step on a journey of healing. It embodies the hope for answers, for treatment, and ultimately, for recovery. As we delve deeper into the realms of medicine, let us carry forward this understanding, honoring the blend of art and science that makes such healing possible.

The discussion of the DSM diagnosis of the client in the case study and the rationale for assigning the diagnosis based on the DSM. People with personality disorders suffer from isolation and loneliness because of the personal limitations that they have. "Clinicians frequently encounter depressed patients experiencing panic or patients of schizophrenia with varying degrees of impairment or a patient exhibiting symptoms of anxiety that could not be clearly labeled as abnormal," (American Psychiatric Association. 2013. p.16).

The DSM diagnosis of the client in the case of loneliness and anxiety disorder. The client in the case study, assigning him to the DSM schizophrenia cannot be ruled out although it might be acute schizophrenia. Related to that, the client may be suffering from post-traumatic stress disorder (PSTD). He suffered emotional and verbal abuse from his father. The pattern of behavior has a long history in his relationship with his classmates at college whom he scorned during the time they were together.

As a result of isolation, loneliness, paranoia, and insomnia, he has developed a defensive mechanism to spend most of his free time playing online games, distancing himself from other people. Even his mother annoys him. The client is experiencing florid symptoms. The dimensional approach of DSM diagnosis has been discovered to help it and chart the course of the disorder, which ultimately distinguishes between normal and abnormal, thus it can be used to screen for mental disorders (Nussbaum. APA, 2013, p. 16).

The rationale for assigning the client with anxiety disorder and schizophrenia is the development of the personality disorder showing in his behavior pattern, which is not consistent. in the process, he consumed himself, and he mentions that he does not need any friends at all. He does not have friends and spends most of his free time gaming online. He has shut down everyone except his mother. He is paranoid and cannot trust anyone. During his school days, he was focused on making to the Dean's list, not in socializing with other students. As a psychotherapist, it is not easy to accurately diagnose a client using DMS diagnosis criteria. It is imperative to learn that even Liebermann and Thomas Insel issued a joint statement, pointing out that the criteria used in clinical practice to diagnose DMS may not offer the credible answers according to the research, "...Looking forward, laying the groundwork for a future diagnostic system that more directly reflects modern brain science will require openness to rethinking traditional categories. It is increasingly evident that mental illness will be best understood as disorders of brain structure and function that implicate specific domains of cognition, emotion, and behavior" (Liebermann and Insel, 2013). This is a strong statement from then the President of the APA and his colleague to make such an observation.

The information that I may need about this client to make an accurate diagnosis based on the DMS diagnosis criteria is about whether he drinks alcohol, is on drugs, his income, his religion if ever he has a religion, and his past. As a psychotherapist, there are some checklists I must employ to get as much information to the client as possible.

The professional practitioner must know his/her limitations but must overcome those limitations by taking practical steps. Being respectful, developing good relationships, reading extensively about diverse cultures and religions, understanding people's ethical values in their contexts and promoting healthy eating, exercise, and education. "The balance may be achieved elegantly with cultural adaptation procedures. We define cultural adaptation as the systematic modification of an evidence-based treatment (EBT) or intervention protocol to consider language, culture, and context in such a way that it is compatible with the client's cultural patterns, meanings, and values," Bernal, G., Jiménez-Chafey, M. I., & Domenech-Rodrígues, M. M. (2009). P. 261. The professional psychology practitioner ought to understand the matrix of cultures and ethical values of his/her patients/clients as alluded to by Bernal, Jimenez-Chafey, and Domenech-Rodrigues.

"The delivery of ethical and culturally consistent therapeutic approaches has continued to challenge practitioners today because of demographic changes throughout the country, professional mandates, and the complex manner in which culture is understood and manifested therapeutically," Gallardo, M. E., Johnson, J., Parham, T. A., & Carter, J. A. (2009). p. 246. When demography changes in society, so does the field of psychology to meet those challenges. Cross-cultural misunderstanding between the providers and the patients can create negative underpinnings that can have lasting impacts on the lives of any given group of people. If the practitioner and the patient have different backgrounds, the language barrier, ethical values, interpretations, and the medical history obtained may be distorted because of the misunderstanding.

OVERCOMING MEDICAL CHALLENGES

In the heart of Zimbabwe, under the harsh glow of fluorescent lights, Dr. Mhlanga stood poised at the precipice of a medical mystery that seemed insurmountable. The air was thick with anticipation, a silent witness to the unfolding drama of life and death. This was not just another day at the office; it was a battle against the unknown, a testament to the resilience and ingenuity of those who dare to call themselves healers.

The context was dire. A young boy, no more than eight, lay writhing on the bed, his body a battlefield for an unseen enemy. His symptoms were perplexing, a constellation of signs that defied easy diagnosis. Fever, rash, and joint pain spoke of many potential foes, yet none fit perfectly the puzzle before Dr. Mhlanga.

The problem was as clear as it was complex. Without a correct diagnosis, the boy's condition could rapidly deteriorate, leading to irreversible damage or, worse, death. The stakes were high, and the margin for error was nonexistent. Dr. Mhlanga knew that the clock was ticking, each passing moment bringing the boy closer to the edge of the abyss.

The consequences of failure loomed large. Misdiagnosis could lead not only to the loss of a young life but also to the erosion of trust in the medical community. In regions where healthcare was a precious commodity, such setbacks could undermine efforts to improve public health outcomes. The ripple effects would be felt far and wide, impacting not just the boy and his family but the community at large.

The solution, while not immediately apparent, emerged from the depths of Dr. Mhlanga's extensive experience and the collective wisdom of his team. They proposed a multidisciplinary approach, combining advanced laboratory diagnostics with a thorough reevaluation of the patient's history and symptoms. It was a strategy that demanded precision, patience, and a willingness to venture beyond the conventional boundaries of medical practice.

Implementation began with a series of specialized tests, each designed to peel away the layers of mystery surrounding the boy's condition. Simultaneously, Dr. Mhlanga initiated a comprehensive review of the patient's medical history, seeking clues that might have been overlooked. Every step was taken with meticulous care, ensuring that no stone was left unturned.

The outcome was nothing short of miraculous. The team's relentless pursuit of answers paid off, revealing a rare, but treatable, autoimmune disorder. The diagnosis was a beacon of hope, a promise of redemption from the clutches of uncertainty.

But what if there had been another way? Alternative solutions have been considered, from broad-spectrum antibiotics to experimental therapies. Each option carried its own set of risks and benefits, a reminder of the delicate balance that defines the practice of medicine. In the end, the chosen path was not the easiest, but the one supported by the strongest evidence, a testament to Dr. Mhlanga's commitment to his patient's well-being.

In recounting this harrowing journey, one cannot help but marvel at the resilience of the human spirit, both in those who seek to heal and those who yearn for healing. Dr. Mhlanga's story is a vivid illustration of the challenges that medical professionals face daily, a reminder of the weighty responsibility they bear.

As the young boy recovered, his laughter filling the once somber words, a sense of accomplishment settled over the team. They had navigated the treacherous waters of uncertainty, emerging victorious against the odds. This was more than a medical triumph; it was a beacon of hope for all who faced the daunting specter of disease.

Dr. Mhlanga, reflecting on the experience, remarked, "In the face of adversity, we find our true strength. It is not the tools at our disposal but our determination to use them wisely that defines our success." His words, simple yet profound, echoed the sentiments of healers throughout the ages.

In the grand tapestry of medicine, stories like these serve as a reminder of the power of knowledge, the importance of empathy, and the indomitable will to overcome. They underscore the essence of what it means to be a "God of Medicine" – not a deity wielding miraculous powers, but a mortal, armed with science and compassion, standing firm against the onslaught of illness and despair.

Thus, the saga of Dr. Mhlanga and his team adds another chapter to the annals of medical history, a testament to the enduring quest to conquer the unconquerable. It is a story of victory, not just over disease, but over doubt, fear, and the unknown. In the end, the greatest challenge is not the malady itself but the journey to overcome it, a journey fraught with peril but illuminated by the light of hope.

Lessons from the Field

In the ever-evolving landscape of healthcare, the journey of a medical professional is fraught with challenges, discoveries, and invaluable lessons. Dr. Mhlanga, through his tireless dedication and insightful experiences, has distilled these into core principles that serve as a beacon for those navigating the complex world of patient care. What follows are the distilled essences of wisdom gleaned from the crucible of medical practice, offering guidance to aspiring healthcare professionals.

Before we delve into the heart of these teachings, it is crucial to understand their foundation. Each lesson is not just a standalone insight but a thread in the fabric of a larger narrative — the narrative of human health and well-being. They are born from moments of triumph and tribulation alike, each a stepping stone towards excellence in medical practice.

In the realm of healthcare, treating symptoms without addressing underlying causes is akin to plugging leaks in a dam without reinforcing its structure. Holistic patient care goes beyond the immediate ailments, exploring environmental, psychological, and social factors that contribute to a patient's overall health. Dr. Mhlanga, drawing from his diverse experiences, emphasizes that understanding a patient's lifestyle, beliefs, and fears is as crucial as diagnosing their physical condition. If the patient's soul is broken, so is his physical.

Studies have consistently shown that holistic approaches can lead to better health outcomes, including reduced stress, improved mental health, and decreased reliance on medications. Patients often recount feeling more understood and valued when their caregivers take a broader view of their health, leading to stronger relationships.

Integrating holistic care into practice means asking the right questions, actively listening to patients, and considering their emotional and social well-being in treatment plans. It involves coordination with other healthcare providers, like nutritionists and social workers, to address all aspects of a patient's health.

THE VALUE OF MULTIDISCIPLINARY TEAMS

The complexity of human health necessitates collaboration across specialties and disciplines. The success in diagnosing and treating challenging cases is largely attributable to the collective expertise of multidisciplinary teams.

Research underscores the benefits of such collaboration, including more accurate diagnoses, more effective treatment plans, and improved patient satisfaction. Testimonials from patients who multidisciplinary teams have treated often highlight the comprehensive care and support they receive.

Building and participating in multidisciplinary teams require open communication, respect for diverse expertise, and a coordinated approach to patient care. It means breaking down silos and fostering a culture of collaboration. Continuous Learning as a Cornerstone

Medicine is a field of constant discovery. Dr. Mhlanga advocates an unyielding commitment to learning, stressing that the day a healthcare professional believes they know everything is the day they become obsolete.

Continuing medical education is mandated for maintaining licensure in many parts of the world, a testament to its importance. But beyond requirements, there is a profound personal and professional fulfillment in staying abreast of the latest research, technologies, and treatment methodologies.

Continuous learning can take many forms, from attending conferences and workshops to engaging in peer discussions and reading the latest literature. It also involves learning from every patient, as each case provides unique insights.

THE POWER OF EMPATHY

Empathy, the ability to understand and share the feelings of another, is perhaps the most powerful tool in a healthcare professional's arsenal. Dr. Mhlanga's experiences underscore that healing begins with empathy, fostering an environment where patients feel seen, heard, and cared for.

Studies have linked empathetic care to numerous positive outcomes, including reduced anxiety and depression in patients, improved compliance with treatment plans, and even decreased malpractice claims. Patients often remember the empathy of their caregivers long after they forget the details of their treatment.

Practicing empathy involves active listening, being present, and showing genuine concern for a patient's well-being. It's about validating their feelings and experiences, offering comfort and assurance.

EMBRACING UNCERTAINTY

Medicine, for all its advances, remains an art as much as a science. Dr. Mhlanga believes that embracing the inherent uncertainties of medical practice is crucial for growth and resilience. It encourages open-mindedness, adaptability, and the humility to seek help when needed.

The uncertain nature of healthcare has been highlighted by global challenges such as the COVID-19 pandemic, reminding professionals of the need to stay flexible and responsive. The most respected clinicians are those who, when faced with uncertainty, proceed with caution, gather more information, and consult with colleagues.

Embracing uncertainty involves acknowledging the limits of one's knowledge and expertise, being transparent with patients about risks and probabilities, and being willing to adjust treatment plans as new information becomes available.

SEAMLESS TRANSITIONS

As we journey from one lesson to the next, it becomes evident that they are interconnected, each reinforcing and building upon the others. The holistic care of patients is enriched by the insights of multidisciplinary teams, which in turn benefit from a commitment to continuous learning. Empathy deepens our understanding and application of these lessons, while embracing uncertainty reminds us to remain humble and adaptable.

In conclusion, the path to becoming a "God of Medicine" is paved with dedication, compassion, and an unquenchable thirst for knowledge. Dr. Mhlanga's lessons from the field are not mere guidelines but beacons, illuminating the way forward for those who aspire to make a difference in the world of healthcare.

THE ROLE OF EDUCATION

In the lush tapestry of contributions that Dr. Sabelo Sam Gasela Mhlanga wove into the field of clinical and spiritual care. As a professor and mentor, his actions reverberated through the halls of academia and into the lives of countless students, shaping the future of healthcare one person at a time. But what was it about his approach to education that left such an indelible mark on health care?

The crux of Dr. Mhlanga's philosophy lies in the assertion that the best health practitioners are not just born but are meticulously crafted through comprehensive education and genuine mentorship. This belief wasn't merely theoretical; it was a principle he lived by, fostering environments where learning transcended the confines of textbooks and leaped into the realm of real-world application.

As we delve deeper into this evidence, it becomes clear that Dr. Mhlanga's methods were transformative. Students who participated in these projects emerged not just as more skilled practitioners but as healthcare professionals deeply committed to the ethos of service and community engagement.

In essence, Dr. Mhlanga's story is a testament to the power of education to transform lives—not just through the dissemination of knowledge but through the cultivation of empathy, community engagement, and a deep-seated commitment to service. As we reflect on his contributions, we are reminded of the enduring truth that the heart of medicine beats not in the pages of a textbook but in the hands of those who serve.

GLOBAL HEALTH INITIATIVES

In the vast expanse of his professional journey, Dr. Sabelo Sam Gasela Mhlanga's dedication to global health initiatives stands as a beacon of hope and innovation. Venturing beyond the classroom's four walls, he embarked on a mission that would leave an indelible mark on the world stage, illustrating a steadfast commitment to confronting global health challenges head-on. This chapter delves into the heart of Dr. Mhlanga's international endeavors, tracing the evolutionary arc of his contributions from their nascent origins to their current standing as pillars of global health improvement.

At the outset, it is crucial to acknowledge the early days of Dr. Mhlanga's global journey. He had optimism and a burning desire to make a tangible difference, and he quickly recognized the vast disparities in healthcare access and quality across different regions of the world. It was a realization that would define his career's trajectory.

Dr. Mhlanga's journey through the landscape of global health initiatives was marked by a keen awareness of cultural and regional variations in healthcare delivery. He understood that each community possessed unique challenges and assets, necessitating tailored approaches to health interventions. This sensitivity to cultural nuances was evident in his work on the HIV/AIDS epidemic.

Why, then, did Dr. Mhlanga persist despite the obstacles? The answer lies in a simple yet powerful conviction: that health is a universal right, not a privilege. This belief fueled his relentless pursuit of equity in health care, driving him to challenge the status quo and advocate for systemic changes.

In reflection, Dr. Mhlanga's contributions to global health initiatives reveal a multifaceted legacy, woven from threads of clinical excellence, cultural sensitivity, and unwavering advocacy for health equity. His story is a compelling narrative of how one individual's passion and determination can spark change, influencing global health policies and practices.

Through his eyes, we are reminded that the essence of health care extends beyond the confines of clinics and that hospitality resides in the hearts of those committed to serving humanity, wherever they may be.

INTEGRATING FAITH AND HEALING

In the labyrinth of human suffering and healing, there exists a profound intersection where faith and medicine converge. Dr. Sabelo Sam Gasela Mhlanga, a venerated figure in the realm of global health, has navigated this complex terrain with an unwavering belief in the synergistic power of spiritual faith and medical science. This chapter explores the essence of this integration, shedding light on how Dr. Mhlanga's spiritual convictions have sculpted his healthcare understanding, especially in healthcare and global health settings.

At the heart of this narrative is the concept of "faith-integrated healing," a term that might seem enigmatic to some. Simply put, it refers to the practice of incorporating one's spiritual beliefs into the medical care process. This approach does not replace traditional medical interventions but complements them, offering a holistic path to healing that honors the mind, body, and spirit.

Dr. Mhlanga's journey into faith-integrated healing was not a sudden epiphany but a gradual realization. Growing up in a community where spiritual leaders were often the first point of contact for the sick, he witnessed firsthand the powerful impact of faith on healing. These early experiences sowed the seeds of a belief system that would later flourish into a comprehensive healing philosophy with God in the picture and understanding the African medicine, coined in spirituality.

Historically, the roots of faith-integrated healing can be traced back to ancient civilizations, where spiritual rituals and medical practices were deeply intertwined. From the shamanic traditions of indigenous African peoples to the healing temples of Asclepius in ancient Greece, the belief in a spiritual dimension of healing has been a universal theme across cultures and epochs.

In the broader framework of modern medicine, faith-integrated healing represents a paradigm shift towards a more holistic approach to healthcare. It acknowledges the limitations of a purely biomedical model and recognizes the role of spiritual and emotional well-being in the healing process.

Dr. Mhlanga's application of this concept in various scenarios, from remote villages in Zimbabwe, Africa to bustling urban centers, demonstrates its universal relevance and adaptability. Whether offering prayers with a family before a challenging surgery or incorporating meditation techniques into treatment plans for chronic illnesses, his practice is a testament to the versatility of faith-integrated healing.

However, misconceptions abound regarding this approach. Critics often dismiss it as unscientific or incompatible with evidence-based medicine. Dr. Mhlanga, through his work, has tirelessly debunked these myths. By demonstrating that faith-integrated healing can coexist with rigorous medical protocols, he has opened his mind to the possibility of a complementary, rather than conflicting, relationship between faith and science.

"Why limit our tools for healing?" This rhetorical question challenges the conventional boundaries of medical practice, urging a more inclusive perspective that embraces the diverse dimensions of human experience.

One striking example is a project in a rural community grappling with high rates of depression with the introduction of meditation and spiritual counseling alongside traditional psychiatric treatments. The whole concept is to understand that God created vegetation, insects, and animals for human existence, for human consumption as well as for human medicine.

In essence, Dr. Mhlanga's fusion of faith and medicine transcends the conventional dichotomy between science and spirituality. It embodies a radical compassion that seeks to heal not just the body, but the soul. His work illuminates a path forward for medicine, one that is enriched by the depth and diversity of human faith.

As we stand on the threshold of a new era in healthcare, the legacy of Dr. Mhlanga serves as a beacon of hope, reminding us that at the intersection of faith and healing, miracles can happen.

Advocacy and Change

Upon the canvas of modern healthcare, a stark picture is painted — one where the divide between the haves and the have-nots is both profound and lethal. The crux of the matter lies in the inequitable access to healthcare services.

What if this chasm continues to widen? The consequences are not merely statistical but are measured in human lives — lives marred by preventable diseases, shortened by lack of medical care, and diminished by the constant struggle for health equity. The ripple effects of this disparity echo through communities, stifling economic development, perpetuating cycles of poverty, and eroding the fabric of societies.

Dr. Mhlanga proposes a multi-faceted approach to bridge this abyss — a blueprint for change that is as pragmatic as it is visionary. Central to his strategy is the empowerment of local communities through education, enabling them to advocate for their health rights. Additionally, he champions the formulation and implementation of policies that prioritize healthcare access for the marginalized. This dual approach aims not only to address the symptoms of the healthcare divide but also to cure its systemic causes.

Evidence of the efficacy of Dr. Mhlanga's approach can be seen in his successful campaign to improve healthcare accessibility in rural regions. The outcomes can be remarkable — increasing vaccination rates, reduced incidence of communicable diseases, and enhanced maternal health outcomes. These tangible results provide a compelling argument for the scalability and replicability that Dr. Mhlanga proposes as solutions for future health care for all.

Yet, the journey to health equity is not without alternative pathways. Some argue for a purely technological solution, leveraging telemedicine and digital health platforms to bridge the gap. While these innovations hold promise, Dr. Mhlanga cautions against viewing technology as a panacea. Without addressing the underlying socioeconomic determinants of health, technological solutions risk widening the divide they seek to close.

In a world where the discourse around healthcare is often polarized and fragmented, Dr. Mhlanga's advocacy offers a beacon of hope. His holistic approach, grounded in the belief that healthcare is a fundamental human right, challenges us to envision a future where health equity is not an ideal but a reality.

"Imagine a world where your zip code does not dictate your health destiny," Dr. Mhlanga often muses, inviting us to ponder a future shaped by equity, compassion, and policy-driven change. Through his relentless advocacy and visionary solutions, Dr. Mhlanga is not just reimagining the landscape of global health; he is actively sculpting it, one policy, one community, one life at a time.

As the narrative of 'God of Medicine' unfolds, it becomes evident that Dr. Mhlanga's story is more than a tale of medical triumphs; it is a manifesto for change, advocating for a world where health is accessible to all, regardless of circumstance. In the face of daunting challenges, his unwavering belief in the power of advocacy serves as a testament to the indomitable human spirit, capable of transforming the very foundations of global healthcare.

CHAPTER FOUR

SCIENCE AND SPIRITUALITY OF HEALING

THE FOUNDATIONS OF MEDICAL SCIENCE

In the vast expanse of human knowledge, few fields possess the transformative power of medical science. Its roots, deeply entwined with the very essence of life and health, stretch far back into history. Yet, it is not the past that captivates us but the future it heralds, a future Dr. Mhlanga navigates with the precision of a seasoned mariner. As we embark on this journey through "The Foundations of Medical Science," let us explore the principles that guide this noble pursuit, principles that are not just academic but profoundly fundamental. At the heart of modern medicine lies a bedrock of scientific principles. These principles, though varied and complex, share a common goal: to understand the mechanisms of health and disease. How does the body maintain its delicate balance? What tips the scale toward illness? These questions form the core of medical inquiry.

Consider, for instance, the principle of homeostasis. This concept, vital yet elusive, underpins our understanding of health. The body, a complex system of systems, constantly adjusts to maintain a stable internal environment. But what happens when this balance is disrupted? Disease ensues. Treating a patient with diabetes, he doesn't merely address the symptoms but seeks to restore equilibrium, guiding the body back to its natural state of balance.

Equally important is the principle of causality, the cause-and-effect relationship that is fundamental to diagnosing and treating diseases. Yet, the practice of medicine is not a solitary endeavor. It thrives on collaboration and differing perspectives. Consider the role of genetics and environment in health. Some argue that our genes dictate our health outcomes, while others point to lifestyle and environmental factors as the key determinants. Dr. Mhlanga sees merit in both perspectives, recognizing that the interplay between genetics and the environment shapes our health in complex, often unpredictable ways.

But let us not forget the power of data and evidence in shaping medical practice. In an era where information is abundant, the ability to sift through data, to distinguish the significant from the trivial, is more crucial than ever. This evidence-based approach ensures that the practice is grounded, not conjecture.

Of course, the language of medicine can be dense, filled with terms that obfuscate rather than clarify. Take "pharmacokinetics," a term that might send the uninitiated reaching for a dictionary. Yet, its concept—how drugs move through and are processed by the body—is essential for effective treatment.

In conclusion, the principles of medical science are not just abstract concepts; they are the tools with which practitioners like Dr. Mhlanga navigate the complex landscape of human health. From the fundamental importance of homeostasis and causality to the nuanced debates over genetics and environment, these principles guide every decision, every treatment. They are bolstered by rigorous evidence yet accessible through clear, straightforward language.

So, what are the key takeaways from our exploration? First, medical science, with its blend of ancient wisdom and modern innovation, is a field of endless discovery. Second, its principles, though rooted in complex science, guide us toward a simple yet profound goal: to heal. Finally, practitioners like Dr. Mhlanga, with their deep understanding and commitment, are not just healthcare professionals but guardians of our most precious asset—our health.

As we close this chapter, let us ponder a question that goes to the heart of medical science: What is health if not the harmony of body, mind, and environment, a harmony that practitioners like Dr. Mhlanga strive to achieve every day?

SPIRITUAL BELIEFS AND PATIENT CARE

In diving into the realm of medicine, one cannot overlook the profound impact of spiritual beliefs on patient care, a domain where Dr. Mhlanga's approach offers a unique and enlightening perspective. This chapter seeks to unravel how Dr. Mhlanga's spirituality intertwines with his healthcare practice, enhancing the healing process and providing a holistic approach to health.

To comprehend the essence of this integration, let us first clarify what we mean by "spiritual beliefs." At its core, spirituality encompasses a sense of connection to something greater than oneself, which can involve a search for meaning in life. It is as personal and diverse as the individuals who practice it, spanning the spectrum from organized religion to personal meditation and reflection.

Delving deeper, spiritual beliefs often serves as a compass, guiding individuals through life's challenges and uncertainties. For many, these beliefs provide a foundation of strength, comfort, and healing. In the context of medicine, spirituality can significantly influence both the patient's and the caregiver's approach to health and illness.

Historically, the link between spirituality and healing is as old as humanity itself. Ancient civilizations, recognizing the intricate bond between body and soul, incorporated spiritual practices into their healing rituals. This tradition, though evolved, continues in various forms across cultures and epochs, underscoring the timeless acknowledgment of spirituality's role in health and healing. Embedding this ancient wisdom within the broader framework of modern medicine, Dr. Mhlanga's practice serves as a testament to the powerful synergy between spiritual beliefs and patient care. By acknowledging the spiritual needs of his patients, he not only addresses their physical ailments but also nurtures their emotional and spiritual well-being. This holistic approach often leads to more profound healing, as patients feel seen and supported in every aspect of their being.

Real-world applications for this integration abound in Dr. Mhlanga's practice. For instance, when counseling patients facing terminal illnesses, he incorporates spiritual counseling, offering solace and helping them find peace and meaning during difficult times. Similarly, in his work with patients battling chronic pain, meditation, and mindfulness techniques are employed as adjunct therapies, providing relief and enhancing quality of life.

However, the interplay between spiritual beliefs and patient care is not without its misconceptions. Some may argue that prioritizing spirituality in medicine could detract from evidence-based practices. To this, Dr. Mhlanga offers a compelling counterpoint: spirituality does not replace medical science but complements it. By integrating spiritual care into his practice, he enriches the healing process without compromising the rigor of scientific medicine.

Indeed, the fusion of spiritual beliefs and patient care represents a confluence of humanity's oldest wisdom with its most advanced scientific achievements. Dr. Mhlanga's approach exemplifies how embracing this duality can elevate patient care, offering a more compassionate, comprehensive approach to healing.

In contemplating the broader implications, one might ponder, could the future of medicine lie in a more integrated approach, where spiritual care is not an afterthought but a fundamental aspect of patient treatment? Dr. Mhlanga's practice suggests a resounding yes. By bridging the gap between the spiritual and the scientific, God does not only heal the body but also soothes the soul, reaffirming the belief that true healing encompasses the whole person.

Thus, as we turn the page on this exploration of spiritual beliefs and patient care, let us reflect on the invaluable lessons from Dr. Mhlanga's practice. In a world where the art of medicine continues to evolve, may we remain open to the profound ways in which spirituality can enhance healing, reminding us of the indelible connection between body, mind, and spirit.

ETHICAL CONSIDERATIONS

In the ever-evolving landscape of modern medicine, Dr. Mhlanga finds himself at a critical juncture, poised between the relentless advance of scientific discovery and the timeless principles of ethical medical philosophy. His journey, emblematic of the broader challenges faced by healthcare professionals, underscores the pressing need to navigate ethical dilemmas with wisdom and compassion. As we delve into this complex terrain, we encounter a particularly poignant issue that exemplifies the ethical quandaries inherent in medicine today.

The conundrum at hand revolves around the use of cutting-edge genetic therapies. These therapies, promising miraculous cures for previously incurable diseases, also pose profound ethical questions. What are the long-term consequences of altering the genetic code? Who gains access to these expensive treatments? Left unchecked, the rush to implement genetic therapies could lead to a future where only the wealthy benefit from the most advanced treatments, exacerbating social inequalities. Moreover, the unforeseen consequences of tampering with the genetic fabric of humanity loom large, Pandora's box of biological uncertainty.

In the face of such daunting challenges, Dr. Mhlanga proposes a solution grounded in ethical principles and scientific rigor. He advocates for a global consortium dedicated to the ethical advancement of genetic therapies. This consortium would not only oversee the development and implementation of these treatments but also ensure equitable access across socioeconomic divides.

Implementing this solution requires a multifaceted approach. Initially, Dr. Mhlanga calls for the establishment of an international ethical framework for genetic research and therapy. This framework would guide scientists and policymakers, ensuring that ethical considerations remain at the forefront of genetic innovation. Following this, he suggests the formation of partnerships between governments, private entities, and non-profit organizations to fund and distribute genetic therapies, thereby democratizing access to these life-saving treatments.

The efficacy of Dr. Mhlanga's proposal is not merely theoretical. Similar consortia have been successful in addressing global health crises, such as the distribution of vaccines in low-income countries. Yet, one might wonder, are there alternative solutions to this ethical dilemma? Indeed, some argue for a laissez-faire approach, letting market forces dictate the development and distribution of genetic therapies. Others propose stringent government control to regulate access and ensure equity. While these alternatives merit consideration, they often fall short in addressing the complex interplay of ethical, economic, and scientific factors at play.

In the final analysis, Dr. Mhlanga's proposal emerges as a balanced, pragmatic approach to navigating the ethical minefield of modern medicine. It underscores the necessity of marrying scientific advancement with ethical governance, ensuring that the march of progress benefits humanity, not just a privileged few.

As we reflect on the ethical considerations shaping the future of medicine, Dr. Mhlanga's journey serves as a beacon, guiding us through the fog of uncertainty. His commitment to ethical practice, balanced with scientific innovation, offers a model for how we might confront the myriad ethical dilemmas that lie ahead.

In this chapter, we've traversed the complex landscape of medical ethics, guided by a steady hand. The story is a testament to the power of ethical consideration in medicine, a reminder that at the heart of every scientific breakthrough and every medical treatment lies a fundamental question of what it means to do good in the world. As we continue our exploration of the "God of

Medicine," let us carry forward the lessons learned from our ethical journey, a cornerstone upon which the future of medicine must be built.

ETHICAL AND MULTICULTURAL SELF-ASSESSMENT

The importance of ethical and multicultural competency in the practice of professional practitioners plays a pivotal role.

To be an ethical and multicultural competent professional practitioner, one must have self-assessment to evaluate one's knowledge, skills, and attitudes on professional competencies to identify personal limitations. Ethical and multicultural competency is fundamental to a professional practitioner because of the diversity and global village we live in, and one must be aware of other cultures, traditions, norms, and religions. It does not mean that the practitioner must know the client's cultures deeply, but just to be aware of, to acknowledge, and to tolerate other people's cultures is fundamental. The professional practitioner must know his/her limitations but must overcome those limitations by taking practical steps. Being respectful, developing good relationships, reading extensively about diverse cultures and religions, understanding people's ethical values in their contexts, and promoting healthy eating, exercise, and education. "The balance may be achieved elegantly using cultural adaptation procedures. We define cultural adaptation as the systematic modification of an evidence-based treatment (EBT) or intervention protocol to consider language, culture, and context in such a way that it is compatible with the client's cultural patterns, meanings, and values," Bernal, G., Jiménez-Chaffey, M. I., & Domenech-Rodrígues, M. M. (2009). P. 261. The professional practitioner ought to understand the matrix of cultures and ethical values of his/her patients/clients, as alluded to by Bernal, Jimenez-Chafey, and Domenech-Rodrigues.

The demographic changes in the country pose some challenges to professional practitioners, but those challenges must be met head-on to bring about stability and professionalism in the field. "The delivery of ethical and culturally consistent therapeutic approaches has continued to challenge practitioners today because of demographic changes throughout the country, professional mandates, 5 and the complex manner in which culture is understood and manifested therapeutically," Gallardo, M. E., Johnson, J., Parham, T. A., & Carter, J. A. (2009). p. 246. When demography changes in society, so does the field of healthcare to meet those challenges. When the country changes demographically, with diverse cultures and an influx of population, history teaches that even knowledge, skills, and attitudes change to meet the challenges from one generation to another. Cross-cultural misunderstanding between the providers and the patients can create negative underpinnings that can have lasting impacts on the lives of any given group of people. If the practitioner and the patient have different backgrounds, the language barrier, ethical values, interpretations, and the medical history obtained may be distorted because of the misunderstanding.

The professional practitioner can eliminate prejudices by learning about the patients' cultural backgrounds, religions, diet, health practices, language, and ethical values. Assumptions about patients' race, ethnicity, culture, gender, and social and language skills should change the paradigm of thinking of a practitioner to meet the needs. (Management Sciences for Health. (n.d.). The provider's guide to quality and culture: Quality and culture quiz. Retrieved November 6, 2018, from: http://academicdepartments.musc.edu/gme/pdfs/Quality%2 0and%20Culture%20Quiz.pdf.

It is imperative to understand your audience/patients as professional practitioners to serve them well and to develop mutual relationships and respect. The five steps towards addressing the limitations to become more ethically and multiculturally competent are as follows:

Awareness of practitioner's cultural values and biases – The professional practitioner must be aware of his/her cultural and ethical values or biases that can limit their professional practice. They must be ready to adjust to their cultural and racial biases to accommodate other human beings who have their own cultures and ethical values.

Awareness of client's worldview – Professional practitioners must be cognizant of his/her clients' worldviews, acknowledge that they have different worldviews and different personalities, and be willing to adjust to aid the patients/clients.

Cultural strategic interventions – Once the professional practitioner intentionally takes some steps to be culturally competent in discharging his/her professional duties, he/she becomes aware of the clients' beliefs, ethical values, religious views, and language. He/she becomes aware of the potential to be the best practitioner in the city, as he/she aims to transcend the nationality, race, religion, beliefs, and prejudices of the clients. (Online Counseling Programs, (2017), 10 Multicultural Factors to Consider in Counseling, https://onlinecounselingprograms.com/blog/multicultural-counseling-model/).

Cultural competence – The professional will be able to assimilate different behaviors, attitudes, skills, and knowledge, cross-culturally to embrace diversity. This will open opportunities to impact society. The culturally skilled practitioner also recognizes his/her limits to his/her competence and expertise.

Cultural Relevance – The professional practitioner will try to be relevant with his/her patients/clients by revolving according to the needs of the clients/patients. Relevance is not complacency, but it is the realization of the changing times and intentionally becoming congruent with the surrounding needs, situations, and circumstances around oneself.

The five steps address the limitations of a professional practitioner to be ethically and multiculturally competent. To be ethically and multiculturally competent, it enhances the practitioner to gain the knowledge, awareness, beliefs, values, and practical skills of diverse cultures, to value, respect, and celebrate diversity but also remaining true to him/herself as a person without losing what he/she is worth.

HOLISTIC HEALTH APPROACHES

In the realm of healing and medicine, Dr. Mhlanga embarks on a path less traveled, intertwining the essence of holistic health practices with the precision of modern medicine. Through this unique approach, he champions the integration of physical, emotional, and spiritual care, crafting treatment plans that cater to the whole person, not just the symptoms of disease. This chapter delves into the core of Dr. Mhlanga's holistic health approaches, unraveling the layers of his methodology to reveal the profound impact of treating the human being as an interconnected system.

Before we journey through the intricacies of holistic health, it's crucial to understand the foundational elements that compose Dr. Mhlanga's approach. These elements are not standalone practices but interwoven threads that, when combined, form a tapestry of comprehensive care.

At the heart of Dr. Mhlanga's philosophy lies the recognition of the mind-body connection, a powerful alliance that shapes our health and well-being. He elucidates how emotional states can directly influence physical health, citing research that links stress to a myriad of health issues, from hypertension to autoimmune diseases. Through mindfulness practices, meditation, and cognitive-behavioral techniques, Dr. Mhlanga empowers his patients to harness the power of their minds to initiate healing in their bodies.

Patients like Maria, who suffered from chronic anxiety and its physical tolls, found solace and improvement through guided meditation sessions and stress management strategies. Her testimony, "I learned to heal my body by healing my mind," underscores the transformative potential of acknowledging the mind-body synergy.

Practically, Dr. Mhlanga integrates these practices into daily routines, encouraging patients to adopt mindfulness as a tool for preventive health care and stress reduction.

"Let food be thy medicine," Hippocrates famously said, a mantra Dr. Mhlanga takes to heart. Nutritional wisdom in Dr. Mhlanga's practice is not about strict diets or fleeting trends but understanding and respecting the body's nutritional needs. He delves into the science of how different foods can either fuel disease or foster health, shedding light on the anti-inflammatory properties of certain diets and the role of gut health in overall wellness.

Success stories abound, like John, who reversed his type 2 diabetes through a tailored nutritional plan that eschewed processed foods for whole, nutrient-rich alternatives.

Dr. Mhlanga's practical application involves detailed dietary assessments and personalized meal plans that align with individual health goals and conditions, making nutrition a cornerstone of his holistic health approach.

In the treasure trove of nature, Dr. Mhlanga finds potent allies for healing. He educates on the efficacy of herbs like turmeric for inflammation, lavender for anxiety, and garlic for cardiovascular health, always grounding his recommendations in scientific evidence and clinical experience.

Patients are often amazed by the power of these natural remedies, like Thandi, who found relief from chronic migraines with a regimen of feverfew and magnesium, avoiding the side effects of conventional medication.

The practical application of herbal medicine in Dr. Mhlanga's practice is careful and considered, with a focus on integrating herbal remedies in ways that complement traditional treatments, ensuring safety and efficacy.

Movement, in Dr. Mhlanga's view, is a medicine for the body and soul. Rather than prescribing generic exercise routines, he advocates for therapeutic movement tailored to the individual's needs and abilities. Whether it's yoga for flexibility and stress relief, for balance and mental clarity, or simply walking in nature, Dr. Mhlanga emphasizes the importance of finding joy in movement.

Case studies, such as Alex, who overcame debilitating arthritis through gentle yoga, highlight the role of therapeutic movement in restoring function and enhancing quality of life.

Dr. Mhlanga's practical approach to therapeutic movement involves not only prescribing specific activities but also educating patients on the benefits of regular, mindful movement as a pillar of holistic health.

Perhaps the most profound aspect of Dr. Mhlanga's holistic health approach is the emphasis on spiritual wellness. Recognizing that spiritual health can manifest differently for everyone, he fosters an environment where patients can explore and nurture their spiritual paths. Whether through meditation, prayer, nature walks, or art, the goal is to connect with something greater than oneself, promoting inner peace and resilience.

The impact of spiritual wellness on physical health is palpable, with patients reporting not only improvements in their medical conditions but also a deeper sense of purpose and contentment.

Dr. Mhlanga's practical application of spiritual wellness is rooted in respect for individual beliefs and traditions, integrating spiritual practices into the holistic health framework in a way that supports each patient's unique journey.

In weaving together these elements of holistic health, Dr. Mhlanga nurtures the seeds of well-being, enabling his patients to thrive in body, mind, and spirit. This comprehensive approach, blending the wisdom of ancient practices with modern medical science, stands as a testament to the transformative power of holistic health. As we explore the depths of Dr. Mhlanga's methodology, it becomes clear that the art of healing is much more than addressing symptoms; it is about cultivating health in its fullest expression, a journey that requires attention to the intricate tapestry of human existence.

CHAPTER FIVE
THE DEBATE: MEDICINE VS. MIRACLES

In a world increasingly defined by scientific breakthroughs and empirical evidence, the age-old debate of medicine versus miracles finds itself at a crossroads. At the heart of this discourse is Dr. Mhlanga, a figure whose healthcare practice stretches beyond the confines of traditional methodologies, embracing the complexities of faith healing and miracles. His perspective offers a unique vantage point, challenging the dichotomies that have long separated the realms of science and spirituality.

The essence of this debate hinges on understanding both medicine and miracles not as opposing forces but as complementary elements within the broader spectrum of healing. Medicine, with its roots in scientific inquiry and evidence-based practice, offers a systematic approach to diagnosing and treating illness. Miracles, or faith healing, transcend the tangible, invoking the power of belief and the supernatural to bring about healing. The significance of exploring this juxtaposition lies in uncovering the potential for a more holistic approach to health and wellness, one that honors both the empirical and the inexplicable.

The rationale behind delving into the dynamics between medicine and miracles is multifold. Primarily, it seeks to illuminate the ways in which these practices intersect, offering insights into how they might coalesce to enhance patient care. Moreover, this exploration aims to challenge prevailing notions about the limitations and capabilities of both medical science and faith healing, proposing a paradigm where each complements the other, broadening the horizons of what is considered possible in the realm of healing.

Setting the stage for comparison, the criteria for analysis encompass efficacy, patient experience, and the role of the practitioner. These benchmarks serve as the foundation for a balanced examination of both subjects, ensuring a comprehensive understanding of their respective impacts on the healing process.

A direct comparison reveals that both medicine and miracles place a strong emphasis on healing, albeit through different means. Medicine relies on tangible interventions, medications, surgeries, and therapies—grounded in scientific research and clinical trials. Miracles, in contrast, draw upon the intangible, the power of prayer, and the belief in divine intervention. Yet, at their core, both seek to alleviate suffering and restore health, highlighting a shared goal despite divergent paths.

The contrast, however, is stark in their methodologies and underlying philosophies. Medicine operates within the realm of the known, guided by the principles of cause and effect. Miracles, on the other hand, venture into the realm of the unknown, predicated on faith and the supernatural. This dichotomy underscores the nuances of each approach, revealing the complexities inherent in their practice.

While visual aids are not applicable in this medium, the vivid imagery of a patient's journey from illness to health can serve as a metaphorical illustration of the interplay between medicine and miracles. Picture a bridge spanning the gap between two cliffs—one representing the scientific, the other the spiritual. This bridge symbolizes the potential for integration, a pathway that allows for the coexistence of two seemingly disparate worlds.

Through this lens, the analysis unveils a broader implication: the potential for a more inclusive approach to healing. One where the rigors of medical science are enriched by the depth of spiritual experience, and where the mystique of miracles is grounded in the realities of the human condition.

In contemporary relevance, this debate mirrors the growing interest in integrative medicine—a field that harmonizes traditional medical practices with alternative healing modalities. The rise of this discipline reflects a collective yearning for a more comprehensive approach to health, one that acknowledges the multifaceted nature of healing.

Dr. Mhlanga's perspective, rooted in both healthcare and an openness to the miraculous, offers a compelling blueprint for the future of healthcare. It challenges the medical community to expand its horizons, to embrace the possibility that miracles, when viewed through the lens of complementarity rather than contradiction, can coexist with medicine. This integration, he argues, holds the key to unlocking new dimensions of healing, where the physical and the spiritual converge, heralding a new era of holistic health.

In essence, the debate between medicine and miracles is not about choosing sides but about bridging divides. It is a call to recognize the value in both, to explore the spaces where science meets spirituality, and to envision a future where healing transcends the boundaries of what is known, venturing into the realm of what is possible.

CRISIS AND COMPASSION: THE GLOBAL HEALTH LANDSCAPE

CONTROLLING EPIDEMICS

In the heart of an African village, cloaked by the dense foliage that whispered secrets of ancient times, a new battle was brewing. It wasn't visible to the naked eye, but its impact was felt deep in the marrow of the community. This was where I, Dr. Sabelo Sam Gasela Mhlanga, found myself armed not with weapons of war but with knowledge, compassion, and an unwavering commitment to healing.

The village, though small, was a bustling nucleus of life, its inhabitants bound by years of shared history and resilience. Together, we formed an unlikely trio, united by a common enemy: an outbreak that threatened to decimate the very fabric of this close-knit community.

The challenge was daunting. An epidemic, swift and merciless, swept through the village, leaving a trail of despair in its wake. Symptoms were initially dismissed as those of common ailments, but as the death toll began to rise, so did the realization that we were dealing with an adversary of a different caliber.

Our approach was multifaceted. We knew that to combat this invisible foe, we needed more than just medicine; we needed to arm the community with knowledge. We initiated an extensive education campaign, using every available medium to disseminate information about the disease, its symptoms, and prevention methods. Naledi mobilized community leaders, leveraging their influence to encourage participation in our programs. Jumo, with his medical expertise, led the charge in treating the afflicted, often working tirelessly through the night.

The results, though slow to manifest, were a testament to the resilience of the human spirit. The tide began to turn. Cases started to decline, and for the first time in months, hope flickered in the eyes of the villagers. We had not only managed to contain the outbreak but had also empowered the community with the knowledge and tools to safeguard against future threats.

Reflecting on this experience brings a mix of emotions. The loss of life was a heavy burden to bear, a reminder of the fragility of human existence. Yet, amidst the sorrow, there were invaluable lessons learned. The importance of community engagement, the power of preventive medicine, and the need for relentless compassion in the face of adversity were underscored in every action we took, every life we touched.

Visual aids, in the form of infographics and charts, were crucial in our educational campaigns. They transcended language barriers, providing clear, actionable information that was accessible to all. These tools were not just aids; they were lifelines, bridging the gap between knowledge and action.

This book, God of Medicine, underscores a fundamental truth: in the war against disease, our greatest weapons are unity, knowledge, and the indomitable human spirit. It connects to the larger narrative of my career, which has been dedicated to not just treating illness but preventing it, empowering communities to take charge of their health and well-being.

As we look to the future, one question lingers: How can we leverage the lessons learned from this outbreak to better prepare for the next? The answer lies not in the pages of medical textbooks but in the stories of communities like this one, which has shown that even in the face of great adversity, humanity can prevail.

So, dear reader, I leave you with this thought: In a world fraught with challenges, what role will you play in forging a path to health and healing?

NATURAL DISASTERS AND HEALTHCARE

Natural disasters, in their ruthless wake, leave scars on the landscape of human existence, challenging the very foundations upon which our societies stand. Among these, the healthcare system faces a Herculean task—rising from the rubble, it must not only heal the wounds of the afflicted but also rebuild itself. This narrative delves deep into the intricate relationship between natural calamities and healthcare. The seeds of this complex interplay were sown at the dawn of civilization itself. When the first communities faced the wrath of nature, be it through floods, earthquakes, or plagues, the need for a system to address the aftermath became evident. These earliest origins of disaster response marked the inception of healthcare's role in recovery, setting the stage for a journey fraught with challenges and triumphs.

As civilizations evolved, so did their response mechanisms. Historical records from various cultures illustrate a tapestry of approaches to disaster healthcare. In ancient times, the Greeks and Romans established military hospitals to care for soldiers injured in natural disasters during wars. Fast forward to the Middle Ages, and we see the establishment of quarantine zones during the Black Plague, a rudimentary yet crucial step in managing health crises post-disaster.

The chronology of significant milestones in disaster healthcare is marked by both innovation and tragedy. The 19th century saw the birth of modern nursing, spearheaded by figures like Florence Nightingale, who revolutionized care in the wake of war and disaster. The 20th century, with its world wars and the Spanish flu pandemic, tested these systems to their limits, leading to groundbreaking advancements in emergency medicine and public health.

Employing mobile clinics and telemedicine provides immediate relief and also lays the groundwork for sustainable healthcare redevelopment in disaster-stricken areas. These efforts are captured vividly in photographs and diagrams, showcasing the transformation of ravaged communities into hubs of healing and hope. The images of makeshift clinics under tents and the smiling faces of those receiving care illuminate the tangible impact of the handiwork.

Cultural and regional variations in disaster healthcare are stark, reflecting the diversity of challenges and resources across the globe. While developed nations often have the infrastructure to implement advanced technological solutions, developing countries rely heavily on community-based strategies and international aid. Recent developments in disaster healthcare reflect a shift towards prevention and preparedness. The integration of climate science into health planning and the use of artificial intelligence in disaster prediction and response are paving the way for a future where the impact of natural calamities on healthcare can be mitigated, if not entirely avoided.

However, this journey is not without its roadblocks. Ethical dilemmas, such as resource allocation during crises and the challenge of maintaining healthcare equity in the face of disaster, pose significant hurdles. The COVID-19 pandemic, a turning point in contemporary disaster healthcare, has highlighted these issues, sparking a global dialogue on how best to navigate them.

The narratives are microcosms of the broader story of disaster healthcare. The experiences, from the trenches of immediate disaster response to the halls of policymaking, underscore the complexities and critical importance of this field. They prompt us to ponder a crucial question: As the frequency and severity of natural disasters increase in a changing climate, how will we adapt our healthcare systems to meet the needs of those in the eye of the storm?

The answer, though multifaceted, begins with stories of a testament to human ingenuity and compassion in the face of nature's fury. It is through these stories that we find the inspiration and wisdom to forge ahead, striving for a world where healthcare stands resilient, ready to face the tempests yet to come.

THE CHALLENGE OF ACCESS

In the tapestry of modern healthcare challenges, access remains a poignant and persistent thread, weaving through the narratives of countless communities across the globe. This chapter focuses on the tireless endeavors that aim to unravel the complex knot of healthcare access in underserved regions. The journey, emblematic of courage and innovation, offers a beacon of hope in the quest for health equity.

In the heart of rural landscapes, where the beauty of nature meets the harsh reality of scarcity, the issue of healthcare access emerges with stark clarity. Here, miles of untamed terrain separate the sick from the healing hands of medicine, a gap widened by a dearth of resources and infrastructure. The consequences of inaction in such a scenario are dire. Without intervention, minor health issues burgeon into life-threatening conditions, preventable diseases claim lives unchallenged, and the cycle of poverty tightens its grip as communities spend what little they have in search of medical help. The ripple effects of inadequate healthcare access extend beyond individual well-being, eroding the very fabric of society.

The first step involved the deployment of mobile health units, buses converted into fully equipped clinics capable of navigating the rugged terrain to offer medical services directly in remote villages. Alongside this, a telemedicine program was established, leveraging the power of technology to connect patients in isolated areas with specialists across the globe. This dual approach promised not only to provide immediate relief but also to lay the foundation for a sustainable healthcare model in these underserved regions.

In areas where the nearest healthcare facility once was a day's journey away, villagers now have access to regular medical consultations. Chronic conditions are managed more effectively, vaccination coverage has expanded, and the overall health of these communities has shown remarkable improvement. These successes serve as tangible proof of the strategy's efficacy, a testament to what is possible when innovation meets compassion.

Yet, the journey does not end here. Alternative solutions continue to emerge, each offering its own set of advantages and challenges. Some advocate for the strengthening of community health worker programs, training locals to provide basic healthcare, thus ensuring sustainability and cultural competence. Others emphasize the importance of public-private partnerships, harnessing the resources and expertise of both sectors to tackle the issue of access head-on.

As we delve deeper into the narrative of healthcare access, questions arise, inviting us to ponder the path forward. How do we scale these solutions to reach every corner of the globe? What role can technology play in overcoming the barriers of distance and resource scarcity? And most importantly, how do we ensure that the human element, the compassionate care that lies at the heart of medicine, is not lost in the process?

Through the eyes of the world, we see the challenge of access not as an insurmountable obstacle but as an opportunity to innovate, to unite, and to heal. The journey to health equity is long, but every step taken is a victory against disparity.

And so, as we turn the page, we are reminded that the story does not end here. It continues in the efforts of countless individuals around the world, fighting to ensure that one day, no matter where one is born, access to healthcare will not be a challenge but a guarantee. The road ahead is fraught with challenges, but with each challenge comes the opportunity to make a difference, to turn the tide in the battle for health equity. The question remains: How will we rise to meet this challenge?

BUILDING HEALTH INFRASTRUCTURE

In the evolving landscape of global health, the construction of sustainable health infrastructure in resource-poor settings emerges as a cornerstone in the battle against healthcare disparity. This chapter unfolds the meticulous process of building health infrastructure, a testament to human resilience and ingenuity.

At the heart of this monumental task lies a simple yet profound goal: to render quality healthcare accessible to all, irrespective of geographical and socio-economic barriers. Imagine communities where the nearest hospital is not hundreds of miles away but within reach. Picture villages where childbirth and common illnesses no longer spell doom due to the absence of medical facilities. This vision, ambitious in its scope, propels the mission forward.

Before a single brick is laid, a myriad of prerequisites must be in place. Essential among these are comprehensive needs assessment, community engagement, securing funds, acquisition of land, and the formation of a skilled project team. Each element, a cog in the larger machine, is critical to the success of the endeavor.

Embarking on this venture requires an understanding of the broad strokes. Initially, one must engage with the community, gauge the needs, and secure buy-in. Following this, the phase of meticulous planning and design takes precedence, where the dreams begin to take a tangible form. The execution stage breathes life into blueprints, transforming them into functional healthcare facilities. Finally, the fruits of labor are realized when these establishments begin to serve the community, an outcome that merits every ounce of effort expended.

Delve deeper, and the complexity of each phase becomes apparent. Engaging with the community involves not just conversations but also building relationships, ensuring that the project reflects the needs and wishes of those it aims to serve. The planning phase demands not just architectural genius but a foresight into the healthcare needs of the future, integrating technology and sustainability into the design.

Execution is where theory meets reality. Challenges abound, from logistical nightmares to unforeseen delays. Yet, it is also a phase replete with opportunities for innovation, requiring a project team that's not just skilled but adaptable and resilient.

Advice to those who dare to walk this path: prioritize sustainability, not just in construction but in operations. Consider the environmental impact, employ local resources, and ensure that the facilities can run efficiently long after the builders have left. A word of caution: do not underestimate the importance of continuous community engagement. The success of a healthcare facility is measured not by its aesthetics but by its acceptance and utilization by the community it serves.

Validation comes when the doors of the new health facility open, and the first patient walks in. Yet, the true test spans beyond the initial flurry of activity. Success is a facility that operates at capacity, with services evolving to meet the changing needs of the community. It is the stories of lives saved, of diseases prevented, and of health education taking root within the community.

Difficulties are inevitable in such ambitious projects. Supply chain disruptions, funding shortfalls, and bureaucratic red tape can stall progress. When faced with such hurdles, flexibility becomes your greatest asset. Explore alternative solutions, engage with partners for additional support, and always keep the community informed and involved. Their belief in the project can often reignite stalled efforts.

The construction of health infrastructure in resource-poor settings is no small feat. It is a venture fraught with challenges yet imbued with immeasurable rewards. Through relentless dedication and innovative approaches, what once seemed an insurmountable task becomes a beacon of hope.

Thus, as we chart the course of building health infrastructure, we are not merely erecting buildings but laying the foundations for a healthier, more equitable future. A future where healthcare is not a luxury but a basic right accessible to all. This journey, while daunting, is rich with the promise of transformation, echoing the enduring spirit of those committed to changing the world, one health facility at a time.

THE POWER OF PARTNERSHIPS

In an era where global health challenges loom large, casting long shadows over communities far and wide, the value of partnerships in healthcare becomes unmistakably clear. Against this backdrop, showcasing the powerful synergy between governments, non-governmental organizations (NGOs), and healthcare professionals is a huge possibility. This collaborative spirit not only bridges gaps but also builds a robust framework for addressing health crises across the globe.

Why, one might ask, are these partnerships so critical in the grand scheme of global health? The answer lies in the multifaceted nature of health challenges today, which demand a response that is equally complex and nuanced. No single entity, acting alone, can hope to address these issues comprehensively. This is the central assertion that guides our exploration.

Consider, for instance, the fight against infectious diseases, a battle that knows no borders. Diving deeper into this evidence, one finds that these collaborations facilitated the deployment of mobile health clinics in remote areas, ensuring that medical care reached those who were previously beyond its grasp. Vaccination campaigns, too, were executed with unprecedented efficiency, thanks to the seamless cooperation between various stakeholders.

However, it would be remiss to overlook the challenges that sometimes accompany such partnerships. Skeptics argue that differing agendas among partners can lead to conflicts, diluting the effectiveness of these collaborations. Indeed, there have been instances where misaligned objectives have caused friction, potentially hindering progress.

In response to these concerns, further clarification is warranted. Successful partnerships are predicated on clear communication, mutual respect, and a shared vision. When these elements are in place, the potential for conflict diminishes, and the collective focus remains squarely on achieving health outcomes.

Moreover, additional supporting evidence underscores the transformative impact of these partnerships beyond immediate health interventions. Educational programs, spearheaded by a coalition of NGOs and local governments, have empowered communities with knowledge about disease prevention and health maintenance, fostering a culture of wellness.

In conclusion, the assertion that partnerships in healthcare are indispensable stands reinforced.

In the grand tapestry of global health, every thread counts, and every partnership matters. It is through these bonds that the world finds the strength to face its most daunting challenges, proving, time and again, that unity is not just a virtue but a necessity. Indeed, in the realm of global health, the power of partnerships is not just a strategy; it's a lifeline.

CHAPTER SIX

INNOVATION IN MEDICINE

PIONEERING RESEARCH

In the heart of Africa, where traditional healing practices intertwine with modern medicine, a revolution in healthcare was brewing. The sun bore down on the bustling city of Bulawayo, a metropolis pulsing with the promise of innovation. With a background as rich and diverse as the minister, professor, and clinical counselor roles he embodied, Dr. Mhlanga was a mosaic of the very best that the fields of spirituality, academia, and clinical practice had to offer.

The challenge that lay before him was as formidable as it was urgent. A new strain of tuberculosis, resistant to conventional treatments, was ravaging communities across the globe. It was a modern-day plague, elusive and seemingly invincible. The world was on edge, desperate for a breakthrough. The key to our future lies in the wisdom of our past.

TECHNOLOGY IN HEALTHCARE

In the realm of healthcare, a revolution is quietly unfolding, driven by the relentless march of technology. As we delve deeper into the integration of technology in healthcare, we uncover a tapestry of innovation that promises to reshape our approach to medicine and patient care.

Embarking on this exploration, we venture into the heart of technological advancements, where each innovation represents a beacon of hope. The significance of these developments cannot be overstated, as they offer new avenues for diagnosis, treatment, and patient engagement.

The era of paper-based medical records is waning, giving way to digital health records (EHRs). These electronic marvels streamline patient information management, ensuring that a patient's medical history is but a click away.

Detail Expansion: EHRs not only improve the efficiency of healthcare providers but also enhance patient safety by reducing medical errors. Their real-time nature allows for quick access to patient data, facilitating more informed decision-making.

Evidence and Testimonials: A study in the Journal of Medical Informatics found that EHRs significantly reduce the time doctors spend on administrative tasks, freeing them to focus more on patient care.

Practical Applications. Hospitals worldwide are adopting EHR systems, leading to dramatic improvements in patient flow and treatment outcomes. For instance, a hospital in Sweden saw a 30% reduction in administrative workload and a 25% improvement in patient treatment times after implementing an EHR system.

As the digital age encroaches upon traditional healthcare models, telemedicine emerges as a key player. It demolishes geographical barriers, allowing patients in remote areas to consult with specialists hundreds of miles away.

Detail Expansion: Through video conferencing, messaging apps, and remote monitoring, telemedicine bridges the gap between patients and healthcare providers. It offers a convenient and cost-effective alternative to traditional in-person visits.

Evidence and Testimonials: A survey by the American Telemedicine Association indicated that 93% of users reported high satisfaction rates with telemedicine services, citing convenience and efficiency as the top benefits.

Practical Applications: Rural communities, previously underserved by the healthcare system, now enjoy better access to medical expertise. A notable example is a tele stroke service in rural Montana, which has drastically improved stroke response times and outcomes.

The rise of wearable technology has ushered in a new era of proactive health management. Devices like fitness trackers, smartwatches, and biosensors offer real-time insights into one's health status.

Detail Expansion: These devices monitor vital signs, physical activity, and sleep patterns, empowering individuals to take charge of their health. The data collected can also be shared with healthcare providers for a more comprehensive view of a patient's well-being.

Evidence and Testimonials: A study published in the American Heart Association's journal highlighted how wearable technology could accurately detect irregular heart rhythms, potentially preventing strokes.

Practical Applications: Wearables have become instrumental in managing chronic conditions such as diabetes, where continuous glucose monitoring devices help patients maintain optimal blood sugar levels.

Artificial intelligence (AI) is transforming the diagnostic landscape, offering unprecedented accuracy and speed. AI algorithms can analyze medical images, identify patterns, and assist in diagnosing diseases at early stages.

Detail Expansion: By learning from vast datasets, AI systems can detect nuances in medical images that might elude the human eye. This capability is particularly beneficial in diagnosing conditions like cancer, where early detection is crucial.

Evidence and Testimonials: Research in the journal Nature Medicine showcased an AI system that outperformed radiologists in detecting breast cancer from mammograms. Practical Applications: AI-driven diagnostic tools are being integrated into clinical workflows, enhancing the precision of diagnoses and tailoring treatment plans to individual patients.

The culmination of technological advancements in healthcare is the advent of personalized medicine. By devising genetic information, doctors can now devise treatment strategies tailored to the genetic makeup of individual patients.

Detail Expansion: Personalized medicine considers the unique genetic, environmental, and lifestyle factors that influence a person's health. This approach enables targeted therapies that are more effective and have fewer side effects. Evidence and Testimonials: The success of personalized medicine is evident in the field of oncology, where targeted therapies have significantly improved survival rates for certain types of cancer.

Practical Applications: Genomic testing is becoming more accessible, allowing for a more personalized approach to treatment across various medical disciplines, from oncology to cardiovascular disease.

As we traverse from one innovative horizon to the next, the interconnectivity between these advancements becomes apparent. Each is a formidable force for change, yet together, they weave a comprehensive network that promises to redefine healthcare as we know it.

The question then arises: Are we ready to embrace this future? A future where technology and healthcare converge to offer a more personalized, efficient, and accessible medical experience.

In this relentless pursuit of better health outcomes, Dr. Mhlanga's vision remains a guiding light. It is a testament to the transformative power of technology in healthcare, serving as a beacon for all those navigating the complex interplay of medicine and innovation.

Through this exploration, we've only scratched the surface of what's possible. Yet, one thing remains clear: in the symphony of healthcare innovation, each advancement plays a critical role, harmonizing to create a melody of improved health and well-being for all.

CHALLENGES OF INNOVATION

In the relentless quest for medical breakthroughs, the journey is fraught with a myriad of challenges that stand between the present and the future of revolutionary healthcare solutions. While the previous narrative celebrated the technological advancements transforming healthcare, it is critical to pivot our focus towards the hurdles that innovation must surmount.

The path to medical innovation is not merely a linear progression from problem to solution. Instead, it is a complex labyrinth that demands navigation through ethical quandaries, the reconciliation of tradition with progress, and the unyielding pursuit of solutions that are as humane as they are groundbreaking.

The primary challenge faced in the realm of medical innovation is the ethical implications that invariably accompany groundbreaking research and implementation. At the heart of this issue lies the question: How do we balance the potential for life-altering treatments with the ethical responsibility to do no harm?

The consequences of overlooking this balance are dire. History is laden with examples where the rush towards innovation led to practices and treatments that, in hindsight, were ethically questionable. The specter of such outcomes looms large, threatening not only the integrity of medical research but also public trust in the healthcare system.

In response to this challenge, a multi-faceted solution emerges, emphasizing the integration of robust ethical oversight in all stages of medical research and innovation. This involves the establishment of ethical review boards equipped with diverse expertise to assess the implications of research projects comprehensively. Furthermore, fostering an environment of open dialogue between innovators, ethics, and the public can ensure that ethical considerations are not afterthoughts but foundational elements of medical innovation.

Implementing such solutions demands a concerted effort from all stakeholders in the medical community. Research institutions must adopt transparent processes for ethical review, while funding bodies should prioritize projects that demonstrate a commitment to ethical standards. Moreover, engaging the public through awareness campaigns and participatory forums can demystify the process of medical innovation, building a bridge of trust between researchers and society.

Evidence of the effectiveness of ethical oversight can be drawn from the field of genetics, where ethical considerations have steered the course of research and application, particularly in the realm of gene editing. The cautious approach, marked by international consensus and strict regulatory frameworks, has prevented premature application of gene-editing technologies, ensuring that ethical dilemmas are addressed before they manifest into real-world consequences.

Yet, ethical oversight is but one piece of the puzzle. Innovation, by its nature, disrupts existing paradigms, often clashing with traditional approaches to medicine. The tension between tradition and progress presents a unique challenge, as it requires balancing respect for established knowledge with the imperative to advance.

The solution to this challenge lies in fostering a culture of co-evolution, where traditional practices and innovative approaches inform and enhance each other. This can be achieved through interdisciplinary collaboration, where practitioners of traditional medicine are engaged in the innovation process, and their insights are valued alongside scientific research.

For instance, the integration of traditional medicinal knowledge with modern drug development processes has led to the discovery of new treatments derived from natural compounds. Such collaborations not only broaden the scope of medical innovation but also ensure that progress is inclusive and respects the diverse cultural contexts within which healthcare operates.

However, the journey does not end here. Alternative solutions, such as leveraging artificial intelligence to predict the impact of medical innovations on societal health outcomes, stand as a testament to the multifaceted approach required to navigate the challenges of innovation.

In conclusion, the road to medical innovation is fraught with challenges that demand a thoughtful, ethical, and inclusive approach. The balance between ethical considerations, tradition, and progress is delicate, yet through collaborative effort, transparent processes, and a commitment to ethical integrity, the pursuit of medical innovation can continue to promise a future where healthcare transcends current limitations, offering hope and healing to all corners of society.

As we ponder the future of medical innovation, let us ask ourselves: Are we prepared to navigate these challenges with wisdom and foresight, ensuring that our pursuit of progress remains anchored in our shared humanity? The answer to this question will shape the future of medicine, guiding us towards innovations that are not only groundbreaking but also just, inclusive, and profoundly human.

THE FUTURE OF MEDICINE

The vista of medicine stretches far beyond the horizon, painted with the bold strokes of innovation and the delicate hues of ethical consideration. As we journey into the heart of this evolving landscape, guided by the vision of pioneers, we find ourselves at the cap of a new dawn. This dawn heralds a future where healthcare is not just about treating illness but preventing it, where personalized medicine becomes the norm rather than the exception, and where technology and human touch merge to create a healthcare experience that is as compassionate as it is efficient.

Imagine a world where your genetic makeup can guide your healthcare plan, predicting potential illnesses and preventing them before they manifest. This is not a mere fantasy but a foreseeable future, thanks to the advancements in genomics and biotechnology. The concept is straightforward: By understanding the genetic predispositions of individuals, healthcare can move from a one-size-fits-all approach to a personalized one. It's a shift from reactive to proactive care, but how does it work in practice?

Take the case of a family with a history of heart disease. In today's world, they might receive general advice on diet and exercise. In the future, however, their genetic profiles could reveal specific risk factors unique to their DNA. Healthcare providers could then tailor interventions, perhaps prescribing medications before problems arise or recommending lifestyle changes backed by genetic insights. This level of personalization could revolutionize preventive care, making it far more effective.

Yet, as we navigate this promising terrain, divergent paths emerge, reflecting a spectrum of perspectives. Some herald these technologies as the pantheon of healthcare's future, while others caution against potential pitfalls. Privacy concerns, accessibility, and the fear of genetic determinism are but a few of the ethical quandaries we must address. Balancing innovation with these ethical considerations requires a nuanced approach, fostering a dialogue that includes not just scientists and doctors but patients and policymakers too.

In this discourse, data plays a pivotal role, offering insights that can help demystify the implications of personalized medicine. Studies have shown that early genetic interventions can significantly reduce the incidence of certain diseases. Yet, questions loom large: Who has access to this technology? How do we ensure it doesn't deepen existing healthcare disparities?

To unravel these complex terms, let's consider 'genetic determinism' - the belief that genes control our health without room for environmental or lifestyle changes. This concept, while overly simplistic, underscores the importance of understanding that genes are not our destiny. They are part of a broader health narrative, one that includes lifestyle, environment, and even our social connections.

As we converge on the conclusion of this exploration, the key takeaways crystallize. The future of medicine is one of boundless potential. It promises a shift towards more personalized, preventive healthcare, leveraging the power of genetic insights. Yet, this journey is fraught with ethical, societal, and logistical challenges. The path forward requires a collaborative effort, one that embraces diverse perspectives and prioritizes the well-being of all individuals.

In the luminous glow of dawn, one question stands out, a beacon guiding our exploration: How do we ensure that the future of medicine is equitable, ethical, and truly transformative? The answer lies in our shared commitment to innovation, tempered by a steadfast dedication to humanity's core values. As we venture into this unknown, let us carry the torch of compassion, curiosity, and courage, illuminating the path toward a future where healthcare transcends the limitations of today, offering hope and healing for all.

CHAPTER SEVEN

LEADERSHIP AND LEGACY

LEADING BY EXAMPLE

Dr. Mhlanga's journey, from a young boy fascinated by the medicinal herbs in his grandmother's garden to the hospitals where he works in America as a health care professional, is a testament to his dedication and relentless pursuit of excellence. His leadership style, deeply rooted in the philosophy of ubuntu "I am because we are" — emphasizes collective success and the well-being of his team and patients alike.

In the broader narrative of the 'God of Medicine, this case study intertwines with the overarching themes of humility, resilience, and the indomitable human spirit. It reaffirms the belief that true leaders are those who, in times of crisis, rise to the occasion, not from a place of authority, but from a place of service to their fellow man.

As we transition from this reflection, one cannot help but ponder the future of healthcare leadership. In a world fraught with challenges, what new paradigms of leadership will emerge? How will the next generation of healthcare professionals draw inspiration to navigate the uncertain waters ahead?

MENTORING THE NEXT GENERATION

One might ask, does mentorship hold such paramount importance in the realm of healthcare? The answer lies not just in the transmission of knowledge but in the cultivation of compassion, empathy, and ethical practice—qualities that define the very soul of medicine. The cornerstone of his mentorship philosophy rests on a simple yet profound premise: to lead by example. Each story, each lesson learned, becomes a thread in the fabric of his mentorship approach.

Delving deeper, it is not merely a transfer of knowledge but an invitation to question, explore, and innovate. Critics may argue that in today's fast-paced, technology-driven world, traditional mentorship models are becoming obsolete. They point to the rise of online learning platforms, virtual simulations, and digital forums as more efficient means of education and professional development. While these tools undoubtedly offer value, counters that they cannot replicate the depth of a mentor-mentee relationship. The nuances of patient care, the art of decision-making amidst uncertainty, and the cultivation of empathy are dimensions that technology alone cannot fully encompass.

By integrating technology with personal mentorship, he creates a holistic learning experience that prepares young professionals for the multifaceted challenges of modern medicine. This approach not only leverages the best of both worlds but also reinforces the irreplaceable role of mentorship in shaping compassionate, competent practitioners.

As this chapter draws to a close, the essence of Dr. Mhlanga's mission in mentoring the next generation becomes crystal clear. It is not merely about imparting knowledge or honing skills but about igniting a flame of passion and purpose that will illuminate the path for future leaders of medicine. While the full extent remains to be seen, one thing is certain—the seeds of wisdom are planted today will blossom into a legacy that transcends time, a legacy where mentorship is revered as the cornerstone of medical excellence.

As the years unfold, significant milestones begin to dot the landscape of his career. Each breakthrough in research, each successful treatment, and each life saved added a layer of depth to his reputation. Awards such as the "Innovator in Medicine" by the Global Health Council and the "Lifetime Achievement Award" by the International Association of Surgeons were not merely accolades; they were beacons of honor, illuminating his dedication and skill.

Throughout different cultures and regions, the significance of recognition in medicine varies greatly. In some societies, such honors are seen as a rite of passage, a formal acknowledgment of a healer's wisdom and contributions. In others, they serve as a rallying cry, inspiring the next generation of medical professionals to strive for excellence and innovation.

In recent years, the advent of new technologies and methodologies has radically transformed the medical landscape. With these changes, the criteria for recognition have evolved, placing greater emphasis on innovation, collaboration, and the ability to adapt to the rapidly changing demands of healthcare.

As we turn the page on this chapter, let us not merely celebrate the awards and honors; instead, let us recognize the enduring impact of the work, the lives saved, the advanced knowledge, and the global community of medical professionals that has inspired this profession. In the end, the true measure of recognition is not found in trophies or titles but in the lasting contributions to the betterment of mankind—a testament to the indomitable spirit of the God of Medicine.

ENVISIONING THE FUTURE

In the heart of every visionary lies a dream so potent, it has the power to reshape the world. This dream extends far beyond the confines of conventional medicine, reaching into a future where innovation, collaboration, and compassionate care converge to redefine healthcare. Imagine a world where the boundaries of medicine are continually pushed forward, not just by technological advancements but through a holistic approach that prioritizes patient well-being above all, a future where healthcare transcends traditional barriers to offer personalized, efficiency, and compassionate care.

Central to Dr. Mhlanga's vision is innovation, a principle that has guided and contributed to health care, medicine, and spiritual care. But what does healthcare innovation truly entail? It's not merely the adoption of new technologies but a fundamental shift in how we approach medical challenges. It involves leveraging the power of artificial intelligence to predict and prevent diseases, harnessing the potential of gene therapy to cure previously incurable conditions, and utilizing telemedicine to bring quality care to remote areas.

Consider the case of a rural health clinic in Africa, transformed through telemedicine to provide vital services to underserved communities. This example illustrates not just the power of technology but the profound impact of innovative thinking in addressing healthcare disparities.

Innovation, however, cannot thrive in isolation. It requires a symphony of collaboration, bringing together minds from diverse fields to solve complex medical problems. Dr. Mhlanga emphasizes the importance of interdisciplinary teams, comprising not just medical professionals but also engineers, data scientists, and ethicists, working together to forge new paths in healthcare.

Reflect on the global response to the COVID-19 pandemic—a testament to the power of collaboration.

Scientists, governments, and organizations worldwide united in an unprecedented effort to develop vaccines, share knowledge, and implement strategies to combat the virus. At the core of Dr. Mhlanga's vision is a commitment to the compassionate care principle that underpins every innovation and collaboration. It's about seeing patients not as cases to be solved but as individuals with unique stories, fears, and hopes. Compassionate care means listening to patients, understanding their needs, and ensuring they feel valued and respected throughout their healthcare journey.

Imagine a hospital where every interaction is guided by compassion, from the design of patient rooms that provide comfort and dignity, to policies that empower patients and their families to be active participants in care decisions. This approach not only enhances patient outcomes but also nurtures a culture of empathy and respect within healthcare systems.

But how do we navigate the uncertainties of the future? A roadmap grounded in continuous learning, adaptability, and an unwavering commitment to the well-being of humanity. It involves staying abreast of emerging trends, being open to new ideas, and fostering a culture of inquiry and innovation within the medical community.

Consider the rapid advancements in genomic medicine, offering new insights into the genetic basis of diseases. By embracing these developments, healthcare professionals can tailor treatments to the individual, marking a significant leap towards personalized medicine.

As we stand on the brink of a new era in medicine, the vision of good health all humanity serves as a beacon of hope. It reminds us that the future of healthcare is not predetermined but is shaped by our actions, our beliefs, and our commitment to making a difference in the lives of those we serve.

In conclusion, the journey towards a brighter future in medicine is fraught with challenges but illuminated by the possibilities of innovation, collaboration, and compassionate care and a call to action for all of us to contribute to a world where healthcare is accessible, equitable, and, above all, human.

As we reflect on the profound insights shared by Dr. Mhlanga, let us embrace the spirit of innovation, the power of collaboration, and the depth of compassionate care. For in these principles lies the path to a future where every individual can attain the highest standard of health and well-being—a future where the dream of the God of Medicine becomes a reality for all.

THE SCALPEL'S EDGE:
MOMENTS OF TRUTH

As we navigate through the intricacies of this journey, it becomes imperative to delve deeper into the realms of healing that transcend the conventional. The narrative thus far has set the stage, inviting the reader into a world where the boundaries between science and spirituality blur, giving rise to an integrated approach towards healing. In this next segment, we explore the sanctuaries of healing that exist beyond the sterile confines of hospitals and laboratories, sanctuaries where the healing touch is complemented by the healing word and where the air is thick not just with antiseptics but with the palpable presence of faith and hope.

In remote corners of the world, where the footprints of modern medicine are yet to tread, lie communities with centuries-old traditions of healing. These are places where the wisdom of the ancients is not relegated to the past but is a living, breathing aspect of daily life. As a traveler and a student of both the scientific and the spiritual, I have had the privilege of professional and non-professional practitioners whose understanding of wellness encompasses the entirety of the human experience – body, mind, and spirit. The lessons learned in these remote sanctuaries of healing have been transformative. They have taught me that true healing often begins when conventional medicine ends. It's in the quiet moments spent listening to a patient's fears, in the shared tears over a seemingly insurmountable challenge, and in the collective prayers for strength and recovery that the essence of healing truly manifests. This realization has been a guiding star in my practice, steering me towards a more compassionate, patient-centered approach to healing.

Furthermore, integrating the wisdom garnered from these traditional healers into my clinical practice has opened new avenues for innovation in medical science. By blending the ancient with the modern, I have embarked on research that seeks to validate the efficacy of traditional healing practices through the rigorous lens of scientific inquiry.

This fusion of knowledge has not only broadened the horizons of medical science but has also provided a beacon of hope for patients for whom conventional medicine had reached its limits. In this chapter, we dive deep into the heart of these lessons, exploring the symbiosis between traditional healing practices and modern medical science. We examine the methodologies of traditional healers, their understanding of disease and wellness, and how these can be harmoniously integrated with contemporary medical practices.

This exploration is not merely academic but is a call to action for the medical community to expand its horizons, to embrace the diversity of healing practices that our world offers, and to recognize that in the confluence of the old and the new lies the potential for groundbreaking advancements in healing. It is a testament to the power of unity – between science and spirituality, between the modern and the ancient, and ultimately, between healer and patient.

As we venture further into this narrative, let us carry with us the lessons of empathy, innovation, and the unwavering belief in the potential for healing that lies within each of us and in the collective wisdom of humanity. The path ahead is rich with possibility, and each step taken is a step towards a more holistic understanding of what it means to heal and be healed.

As we venture deeper into the heart of 'God of Medicine,' we find ourselves navigating the intricate mosaic of human experience, where each tile represents a unique story of struggle, hope, and redemption. In this chapter, we delve into the essence of what it means to heal, exploring the delicate balance between the empirical and the ethereal, between the tangible medicines derived from the earth and the intangible healing that emanates from a place beyond our understanding. It is here, in this sacred space, that the true artistry of healing reveals itself.

My journey has taught me that to heal one another must first understand the depth of their suffering. This understanding cannot be achieved through clinical detachment but through a profound empathy that transcends the boundaries of our own experiences. It is a lesson I learned early in my career, in the bustling wards of a hospital where the air was thick with despair and hope in equal measure. I recall the case of a young woman, her body wracked with disease, her spirit shattered by the relentless assault of pain. Conventional medicine had reached its limits, offering no solace to her suffering. It was in her eyes, the silent pleas for relief, that I found my resolve tested.

Drawing upon the wisdom from God, coupled with the knowledge acquired through years of clinical and spiritual training, I embarked on a journey with her that would challenge the very core of my expertise. Together, we explored avenues of healing that bridged the gap between science and spirituality, employing not just professionalism but also practices grounded in meditation, prayer, and the laying on of hands. The transformation was not immediate, nor was it easy. It required faith, patience, and an unwavering commitment to the belief that healing is as much about the soul as it is about the body.

This experience, among countless others, solidified my conviction in the holistic approach to healing. It underscored the importance of listening not just to the words of those who seek our help but to the unspoken language of their hearts. In the realm of true healing, every gesture, every silence, every tear holds a clue to the path of recovery. It is a path fraught with challenges, yes, but also rich with the potential for transformation.

As we move forward in this narrative, we encounter stories of miraculous recoveries that defy conventional explanation, stories that reaffirm our belief in the power of faith and the resilience of the human spirit. These are not mere anecdotes meant to inspire; they are testaments to the potential that lies within each of us to transcend our limitations and to touch the divine, however we may conceive it. In the pages to come, we will explore the landscapes of healing in all their complexity, from the biochemistry of our bodies to the metaphysics of our souls.

We will meet individuals who, in their darkest hours, found light not through the prescriptions of man but through the grace of something greater. Through these encounters, we will come to understand that the journey of healing is not just about restoring health but about reclaiming the wholeness of our being. So, let us continue with hearts open and minds attuned to the myriad ways in which the God of Medicine manifests in our lives. For in every breath, in every heartbeat, lies the potential for healing, a promise of renewal that sustains us through the trials and tribulations of our mortal journey.

WHISPERS OF THE FORGOTTEN STETHOSCOPE

In this ongoing narrative of healing where faith and medicine converge, Dr. Sabelo Sam Gasela Mhlanga's journey embodies a profound exploration into the depths of human resilience and the capacity for recovery. His experiences, rich with the wisdom gleaned from both the clinical and spiritual realms, reveal the intricate tapestry of life, where every thread is interwoven with the delicate strands of belief, hope, and the enduring power of the human spirit. Amidst the clinical precision of medical science, Dr. Mhlanga discovered an essential truth: that true healing often begins where conventional medicine reaches its limits. It is in these liminal spaces, the thresholds between despair and hope, sickness and health, that he found his calling, not just as a healer but as a guardian of the human spirit.

His method, a blend of cutting-edge medical treatments with the physicians and the nurturing touch of spiritual counsel, has redefined the boundaries of healing, proving time and again that when the mind, body, and spirit are treated as a unified whole, miraculous recoveries are possible. Through a meticulous process of medical evaluation, coupled with deep, empathetic engagement with the young man's spiritual and emotional landscape, Dr. Mhlanga was able to unlock the door to healing. It was a journey that transcended the mere alleviation of symptoms, fostering a profound renewal of spirit and a rekindling of hope. Yet, the journey of healing is not a solitary endeavor. It is a collaborative pilgrimage, a shared quest for wholeness that binds healer and patient together in a mutual pursuit of wellness.

Dr. Mhlanga's practice has become a sanctuary, a place where the weary and the wounded can find refuge and restoration. Here, amidst the sterile precision of medical instruments, lies a space where the human heart is acknowledged, where the stories of suffering and survival are honored, and where every individual is seen, heard, and valued. His true legacy is written in the lives of those he has touched, in the silent prayers of gratitude whispered by families reunited with their loved ones, in the smiles of those who had forgotten what it meant to live without pain.

It is a legacy of compassion, of unwavering faith in the potential for healing that resides within every human being. In the grand tapestry of Dr. Mhlanga's career, each thread represents a life intertwined with his own, each color a story of pain, hope, and healing. As we continue to weave through the narrative of his journey, we are reminded of the profound truth that in the art of healing, the greatest medicine is often found not in a pill or a procedure, but in the human connection, in the shared belief in the possibility of a better tomorrow, and in the unwavering commitment to walk together, hand in hand, towards the dawn of healing.

In the sacred corridors of healing, where science and spirit intertwine, the journey of a healer begins, where each day unfolds as a testament to the miraculous interplay between divine intervention and medical science. This journey into medicine is punctuated with tales of triumph and tribulation, each patient's story a sacred trust, and every diagnosis a puzzle that beckons the marriage of science and intuition. Beyond the clinical encounters lie the broader canvases of community health projects, global health initiatives, and the integration of faith and healing, where my roles as a teacher, mentor, and advocate unfold. This narrative delves into the heart of medical science, exploring its foundations while embracing the spiritual beliefs that have guided my approach to patient care. The ethical dilemmas, the holistic health approaches, and the ongoing debate between medicine and miracles form the crucible in which my medical philosophy has been forged.

MODERN MEDICINE IN SYNCH WITH GOD'S PURPOSE

When aligned with God's purpose, it becomes a profound testament to the harmony between divine wisdom and human innovation. God's purpose in healing encompasses restoration, compassion, and the promotion of well-being for all creation. Modern medicine, as an extension of this divine intent, has the potential to serve humanity while honoring the Creator's principles.

The advancements in medicine—be it through cutting-edge technologies, life-saving treatments, or groundbreaking research—are reflective of God's gift of intellect and creativity to humanity. These innovations are not merely human achievements but manifestations of divine grace, enabling people to address complex health challenges. Vaccines, antibiotics, and surgical procedures all demonstrate the miraculous blend of divine inspiration and human effort.

However, staying in synch with God's purpose requires that modern medicine maintain its ethical foundation. Compassion, empathy, and a focus on holistic care must remain central. The principle of "do no harm," deeply rooted in medical ethics, resonates with the divine command to protect and nurture life. It emphasizes the sanctity of life, and the responsibility entrusted to medical professionals.

Integrating spiritual care into medical practice further aligns it with divine purpose. Addressing not only physical ailments but also the emotional and spiritual needs of patients foster a deeper sense of healing and connection. It acknowledges the truth that humans are not merely biological beings, but also spiritual entities created in God's image.

Collaboration between faith and science can elevate modern medicine, ensuring it fulfills its highest potential. By seeking wisdom through prayer, reflection, and ethical considerations, humanity can harness medical advancements to serve God's greater plan. This approach nurtures a world where medicine is not only a tool for healing but also a bridge to divine love and care.

Impact & Effects of Contemporary Medicine on Human Health .... The impact of contemporary medicine on human health is profound and multifaceted. On the one hand, it has led to remarkable advancements that have transformed healthcare, improving life expectancy and quality of life. On the other, it presents challenges and ethical considerations that must be carefully navigated.

Contemporary medicine has significantly reduced mortality rates through innovations such as antibiotics, vaccines, and advanced surgical techniques. Chronic diseases, once considered untreatable, are now manageable, allowing individuals to lead longer, healthier lives. Breakthroughs in genetic research and personalized medicine have further refined treatment approaches, tailoring them to individual needs and conditions.

However, the effects of modern medicine are not without complexity. The reliance on pharmaceuticals has, in some cases, led to issues like drug resistance, dependency, and side effects. Over-medicalization, where natural processes are treated as illnesses, raises concerns about the balance between intervention and allowing the body's innate healing abilities to function.

The rise of technology in medicine, while a boon, also brings challenges. Telemedicine and artificial intelligence have improved accessibility and diagnostic accuracy but may risk depersonalizing healthcare. Maintaining the human connection in medicine is crucial to preserving compassion and empathy, which are vital components of healing.

Environmental and societal impacts also merit attention. The production and disposal of medical waste

CHAPTER EIGHT
MEDICAL ANTHROPOLOGY

Medical Anthropology is the study of human health, disease, treatment, prevention, and health care systems. This includes the scientific study of humanity, human behavior, human biology, culture, linguistics, and societies in the past, present, and future. Medical Anthropology investigates and examines people's health and illness in the context of understanding their bodies and souls. The branches of Medical Anthropology, such as Biomedical, Sociomedical, and Epistemology, are explored. Chapter Five of the book discusses Medical Anthropology and Archeology theory and methods, Empirical methods, and Biocultural factors that impact human health. "Anthropology is the study of the origin and development of human societies and cultures. Culture is the learned behavior of people, including their languages, belief systems, social structures, institutions, and material goods. Anthropologists study the characteristics of past and present human communities through a variety of techniques. In doing so, they investigate and describe how different peoples of our world lived throughout history."[28]

28

https://education.nationalgeographic.org/resource/history-branches-anthropology, (Accessed May 25, 2022).

MEDICAL ANTHROPOLOGY - BIOMEDICAL

The biomedical stems from the biocultural aspects that shape certain populations that respond to modern medical interventions. It considers human biology and health, necessitates the skeletal, the molecular and the population of certain group of people and particular diseases. The major research in the biomedical field includes neuroscience, cancer biology, regenerative medicine, and reproductive biology. Biomedicine contends that illness is caused by deviations from universal biological norms into biological abnormality. "As the world becomes increasingly multicultural and mobile, combining cultural understanding with biomedical knowledge is growing in importance. Because of this, biomedical anthropology focuses not only on molecular or cellular mechanisms of pathology and the transmission and the dissemination of diseases but also bio bio-sociocultural factors that affect health outcomes for both individuals and the populations."[29] Biomedical anthropology enhances the understanding of anthropology, human health, illness, and human biology, including sociocultural and cross-cultural perspectives. It examines culture, race, ethnicity, class, gender, and inequality and emphasizes effective cross-cultural communication, which is vital in human ethnography.

---

[29] https://www.petersons.com/blog/biomedical-anthropology-a-degree-for-the-future-of-medicine-and-science/, by Ben, (November 29, 2017).

MEDICAL
ANTHROPOLOGY – SOCIOMEDICAL

Sociomedical science covers evolutionary medicine, species ethnography, disease ecology, human disease, health, medicine, and human ecology. All this is to address human health to restore humanity and dignity, not to succumb to catastrophic human demise. The field addresses the social, historical, cultural, psychological, and economic realms of human health to advance social justice and to improve human health. Sociomedical aims to enhance public health and to explore sexuality, urban health, aging, homelessness, drug use, and mental health and health care access to all. Sociomedical is connected to Social Sciences, addressing historical, social, cultural, economic, psychological, and archeological issues that influence and affect human outcomes. Sociomedical can develop strategies that can help to make research on education, address health inequality, social justice, and other human social services. Social Sciences include education, housing, poverty, transport, health care organizations, and the environment that affect the population. Some of these factors enable and prevent loss of lives in society.

Some of the major focuses of social medicine are outlined by the medical anthropology of the causes, the spread, the treatment, and the prevention of diseases and illnesses.

MEDICAL ANTHROPOLOGY - EPIDEMIOLOGY

Public Health's thrust is to protect the communities where they live, play, learn, work, and thrive. Basically, Epidemiology is the study of human health issues, and it deals with the incidents, control of diseases, distribution, and health incentives and services to communities. Human diseases and disorders spread along the frameworks of cultural and social structures, hence the need for Epidemiology techniques to curb diseases. Epidemiology is fundamental in shaping human and public health to prevent catastrophic healthcare disasters.

Epidemiology enhances the fundamentals of developing clinical methodologies and research to improve health care systems. "Major areas of epidemiological study include disease causation, transmission, outbreak investigation, disease surveillance, environmental epidemiology, forensic epidemiology, occupational epidemiology, screening, biomonitoring, and comparisons of treatment effects such as in clinical trials. Epidemiologists rely on other scientific disciplines like biology to better understand disease processes, statistics to make efficient use of the data and draw appropriate conclusions, social sciences to better understand proximate and distal causes, and engineering for exposure assessment,"[30] Epidemiology plays a pivotal role in healthcare systems for research and to the particular group of people's understanding of their health, culture, diseases, treatment and prevention.

Every society or community needs Epidemiology research to curb human diseases and the prevention to survive. "Epidemiological studies are aimed, where

---

30

https://en.wikipedia.org/w/index.php?search=&title=Special:Sear ch, (Accessed February 10, 2023).

possible, at revealing unbiased relationships between exposures such as alcohol or smoking, biological agents, stress, or chemicals to mortality or morbidity. The identification of causal relationships between these exposures and outcomes is an important aspect of epidemiology"[31]

---

[31] Ibid.

ARCHEOLOGY & BIOCULTURAL

Archeology is a pivotal anchor in the understanding of medical anthropology about human society and people's lives. Archelogy is a glue entity that puts puzzle pieces together of human life as a scientific trajectory and ethos that governs humankind. It is clearly to be understood that "Archaeology is the systematic study of the human past through material remains. Archaeologists examine diverse remnants of human actions through excavation, recovery, and material analyses. Cultural systems through time and space are reconstructed by examining ancient social, political, religious, and economic systems through both a regional and comparative perspective. As such, archaeologists rely on a plethora of methods and techniques avenues including specific artifact analyses (bones, ceramics, lithics, paleobotany) as well as geographic information systems (GIS)."[32] In the same vein, archeology is combined with biological anthropology to augment the accurate results of tests and evaluation of the data gathered using all kinds of reliable tools and instruments such as 14 carbon dating.

As such, "Biological anthropology is the study of humans and non-human primates from an evolutionary and biocultural perspective. It is the most humanistic of scientific disciplines due to the complex cultural organization, institutions, and symbolism associated with human populations, yet the most biologically oriented humanistic discipline due to the unifying emphasis on evolutionary theory. Biological anthropologists' study diverse subject matter including the behavior and biology of non-human primates, the evolution of human populations based on fossil and genetic data, and the health, well-being, and resiliency

---

[32] https://soan.gmu.edu/about-overview/anthropology/archaeology, (Accessed March 6, 2023).

of contemporary populations."[33] To complement biological archeology, there is also bioarcheology, which focuses on the studies of skeletal remains. It entails that both biological anthropology and bioarcheology are tapping their guidance from cultural anthropology and evolution biology. By the same token, biocultural studies zero in on the interaction between biological and cultural phenomena, which is foundational in informing research institutions about the past remains of humans and animals to learn from the past societal way of life. If a group of people or society forgets its past, it is ultimately denying its destiny and renouncing or denouncing its future.

---

[33] Ibid.

ARCHEOLOGY THEORY AND METHODS

The archeology theory and methods used in bioarcheology, cultural archeology, and medical anthropology are meant to determine the past lifestyles, culture, food, tools, and other things used in the past to inform modern archeology. "Bioarcheologists use the methods of skeletal biology, mortuary archaeology, and the archaeological record to answer questions about the lives and lifestyles of past Populations"[34] The archeological theory is the interaction and the different intellectual frameworks in which archeologists interpret archeological data and analyze them for scholarly research. There are three types of archeology. "Medieval archeology is the study of post-Roman European archaeology until the sixteenth century. Post-medieval archaeology is the study of material culture in Europe from the 16th century onwards. Modern archaeology is the study of modern society using archaeological methods …"[35] In the field of archeology, there are methods employed to gather data. "Archeologists use several methods to establish relative chronology including geologic dating, stratigraphy, seriation, cross-dating, and horizon markers… Geologic dating. Geologists study the earth and the natural forces that are involved in changes that take place."[36] All this is done to determine the age and the dates of the remains left behind.

---

[34] Ibid.
[35] https://soan.gmu.edu/about-overview/anthropology/archaeology, (Accessed March 7, 2023).

[36]

https://www.google.com/search?q=archaeological+method+and+theory, (Accessed March 7, 2023).

BIOCULTURAL IMPACT
ON HUMAN HEALTH

The biocultural impact on human health goes beyond and above human imagination. Biocultural is research on human biology, culture, lifestyle, and medical ecology that is composed of social, cultural, and behavioral variables in the research designs aimed at finding accurate data about the past. "Valuable models for studying the interface between biological and cultural factors affecting human well-being. Two models of biocultural research predominate in health studies: one which integrates biological, environmental, and cultural data, and a second, more segmented model in which biological data are primary and data on culture and environment are secondary."[37] The biocultural impact on human health has a tremendous effect, and it needs to be learned, preserved, and understood in the context of human spirit, dignity, and mutual respect.

It is imperative and fundamental to understand that history, culture, and humanity have been put on this planet for a purpose and must be understood from religious, spiritual, and cultural perspectives. "A biocultural approach provides an emerging framework for clarifying the mechanisms that connect water security to human health and wellbeing. Five basic tenets of the biocultural approach are outlined: The focus on the local, the centrality of culture, the notion of embodied disadvantage, a concern with proximate mechanisms to test theorized pathways..."[38]

---

[37] Ann McElroy, Medical Anthropology Quarterly, *International Journal for the Analysis of Health*, September 1990, https://anthrosource.onlinelibrary.wiley.com/, (Accessed March 7, 2023).

[38] Alexander A. Brewis, et al, WIREsWATER,

Health is a human right and in the same vein, health care is a human right because every human being deserves to enjoy health care as a fundamental right and must be maintained and protected. Human health drives the nation's economy, industry, commerce, tourism, and human resources. The unhealthy nation is doomed to destruction because it does not have any potential, hope, or a future. Quality medical care is responsible for life expectancy in the nation. Many factors can improve life expectancy, including education, nutrition, hospitals, and health care systems. Human services, social goods, and health care systems are the determinants of how the government impacts human health in the country.

Environmental degradation, air pollution, food insecurity, poor education systems, poor nutrition, poor transportation, and inadequate housing facilities can derail any country on its economic development. Community development and healthcare systems are engineered, propelled, and maintained by government entities and anchored by the local government branches.

---

https://doi.org/10.1002/wat2.1440, April 15, 2020, (Accessed March 7, 2023).

CONCLUSION

In conclusion, the God of Medicine book captures the essence of the belief that God is the creator and the source of life, vegetation, animals, the galaxy, the universe at large, and humanity. As such, all medicine, healing, the art of telepathy, diseases, and treatments were well discussed. Medical research, the methods of treatment, and the prevention of diseases in this generation and the next generation. The integrated faith and healing were explored in this book with science and spirituality. My journey into counseling and spiritual ministry was an expansion. It was an acknowledgment that true healing transcends the physical, touching upon the emotional and spiritual wounds that often lie at the heart of our ailments. In the vast expanse of human knowledge, few fields possess the transformative power of medical science. Its roots, deeply entwined with the very essence of life and health, stretch far back into history. I hope this book has inspired you to serve your community to bring good health to all, especially those who are underprivileged. It is imperative to know and understand that God is the God of Medicine /and healing.

The tapestry of the book, 'God of Medicine' brings God into the right perspectives to enlighten humanity about the real source of life, health, and medicine. Treatment and prevention of diseases is humanity's mandate to treat each other to live healthy lives in their lifetime. Human health drives the nation's economy, industry, commerce, tourism, and human resources. Over-medicalization, where natural processes are treated as illnesses, raises concerns about the balance between intervention and allowing the body's innate healing abilities to function.

BIBLIOGRAPHY

Arthur Kleinman, *Experience and its Moral Modes: Culture and Human Conditions and Disorder*, The Tanner Lectures on Human Value, Stanford University: April 13-16, 1998.

Bryan J. Good, *Medicine, Rationality and Experience*, New York: University of Cambridge   Press, 1994.

Cheryl Mattingly, Moral Laboratories: Family Peril and the Struggle for Good Life, Berkeley, CA: University of California, Press, 2014.

John Calvin, *Commentary on Genesis, Commentaries on the First Book of Moses*, vol. 1 Grand.

Kenneth A. Mathews, *Genesis 1-11:26*, The New American Commentary, vol. 1A Nashville: Broadman & Holman, 1996.

Gordon J. Wenham, *Genesis 1-15*, Word Biblical Commentary, vol. 1 (Waco, TX: Word,   1987.
Sam B. Puckett and Alan R. Emery, *Managing AIDS in the Workplace* Reading, MA: Addison, 1988.

REFERENCES

https://www.who.int/health-topics/severe-acute-respiratory-syndrome#tab=tab_1

https://my.clevelandclinic.org/health/diseases/15014-malaria, (Accessed September 5, 2022).

National Library of Medicine: *National Center for Biotechnology, Article,* https://pubmed.ncbi.nlm.nih.gov/9892288/, 2018, (Accessed August 30, 2022).

Scheper, Hugh, and Lock, *ANTH 215 A*, Lecture 1, 2018, p.33.

Messinger, *ANTH 215 A*, Lecture 3, January 22 and 24, 2018, p. 2,3,4.

Messinger, Lecture 3, 22, 224, 2018, p. 8 Rapids: Baker, 1996), 97

Seth, Messinger, *ANTH 215 A*, Lecture 3, 22, 2018, p. 21.

Seth Messinger, Lecture 4, January 29, 2018, p. 29.

Hamilton, *The Book of Genesis*, 139.

Leupold, *Exposition of Genesis*, 184.

(Online Counseling Programs, (2017), 10 Multicultural

Factors to Consider in Counseling,
https://onlinecounselingprograms.com/blog/multicultural-counseling-model/).
https://education.nationalgeographic.org/resource/history-branches-anthropology, (Accessed May 25, 2022).

https://www.petersons.com/blog/biomedical-anthropology-a-degree-for-the-future-of-medicine-and-science/, by Ben, (November 29, 2017).

https://en.wikipedia.org/w/index.php?search=&title=Special:Search, (Accessed February 10, 2023).

https://soan.gmu.edu/about-overview/anthropology/archaeology, (Accessed March 6, 2023).

https://soan.gmu.edu/about-overview/anthropology/archaeology, (Accessed March 7, 2023).

https://www.google.com/search?q=archaeological+method+and+theory, (Accessed March 7, 2023).

Ann McElroy, Medical Anthropology Quarterly, *International Journal for the Analysis of Health*, September 1990, https://anthrosource.onlinelibrary.wiley.com/, (Accessed March 7, 2023).

Alexander A. Brewis, et al, WIREsWATER, https://doi.org/10.1002/wat2.1440, April 15, 2020, (Accessed March 7, 2023).

www.ingramcontent.com/pod-product-compliance
Lightning Source LLC
Chambersburg PA
CBHW061653120626
46550CB00003B/925

* 9 7 9 8 9 8 9 9 2 2 1 5 4 *